DEATH AND DYING:

Views from Many Cultures

EDITED BY

RICHARD A. KALISH

Baywood Publishing Company, Inc.

Library of Congress Catalog Card Number: 78-67784

ISBN Number: 0-89503-012-8

Libary of Congress Cataloging in Publication Data

Main entry under title:

Death and dying: views from many cultures

    (Perspectives on death in human experience series; 1)
    Includes bibliographical references.
    CONTENTS: Death in preliterate communities:
Achte, K. Death and ancient Finnish culture. Huber, P. S.
Death and society among the Anggor of New Guinea. Jones,
R. L. Religious Symbolism in Limbu death-by-violence. [etc.]
    1. Death—Addresses, essays, lectures. 2. Funeral rites
and ceremonies—Addresses, essays, lectures. 3. Mourning
customs—Addresses, essays, lectures. 4. Bereavement—
Addresses, essays, lectures. I. Kalish, Richard A. II. Series.
GT3150.A57   1979   393'.08   76-67784
ISBN 0-895030-012-8

Preface

The only certainty for everyone who is born is that death will occur. This is an event, an experience, that is shared by people throughout history, throughout the world, and—if there is life on other planets—most probably throughout the universe. It is something that human beings share with all other species and, if you wish to extend the concept, to all other forms of life.

But we differ from other forms of life because we can anticipate our deaths. We can plan for dying and death, develop ceremonies and rituals that affect the dying, the dead, and the survivors, and worry about death. We are probably the only living things on earth that think about death in advance of the event, and the knowledge that some day we will die is a constant influence on how we live each day. Consider how your life might be different today if you believed that your death would occur in six years or in 60 or in 600 years. Or how would you live today if you believed that you would be alive on earth 600,000 years from now?

Each society has developed roles, beliefs, values, ceremonies, and rituals to integrate death and the process of dying into the culture as a whole and to help individuals cope with the mysteries and fears of death. And each individual must adapt these folkways to his or her own needs, wants, personality, and situation. While aimed at being adaptive, these folkways can also have some harmful effects on certain members of the society.

One familiar way to deal with the fears and wonders about death is to believe that death is not an end, not extinction, but a rite of passage to another existence. Sometimes this existence does not differ very much from the present existence, except that it is usually more pleasant; sometimes this existence is seen as a kind of eternal peace, even an eternal sleep. Once again it is culture that shapes what each individual believes to be the meaning of death.

Culture shapes not only the meaning of death, but also how we die; and one unanswered question is whether culture can bring about a meaning of death that enables people to go through the dying process without fear. Some people believe that fear of death and, therefore, of dying is universal and can be reduced but not eliminated by culture; others feel that the proper cultural values can take all the sting out of death.

A great deal has been written about death and dying in cultures around the world and throughout history. Much of what we know about earlier cultures we know because of death: through burial sites and tombs, we have uncovered a great deal of the world's past. Since death occurs in all cultures, we can also make certain comparisons across cultures in the ways in which they handle funerals, burials, sickness, family relationships, and religious beliefs.

In this volume we have brought together a variety of kinds of studies. Part One describes death and dying in cultures that most of us know little or nothing about. They are isolated communities, affected by technological change but still adhering to modifications of old values.

Part Two focuses on North America and its cultures, considerably closer to home and yet often unrecognized as having their own histories and traditions that mold the feelings and responses to dying and death of their members. Again we have taken an historical perspective, since viewing a culture across time can enhance the understanding of what is happening today and of why it is happening.

The final part describes wars and disasters, two much-discussed events that are not often viewed in terms of the role of death and dying, even though much of the impact of these events is exactly that. The final chapter is one that I particularly prize because it shows how easily we can be manipulated to justify behavior that at another psychological level we would disdain. Perhaps each of us carries the seeds of anger, fear, and destruction, perhaps circumstances would make executioners of us all.

Thus, this volume views death and dying across time and across cultures, ranging from contemporary North America to historical Spain and to a New Guinea that seems almost outside of time. And, to understand death and dying, the various chapters focus on observed behavior, poetry and songs and stories, informants, and history books.

Richard A. Kalish
Berkeley, California
May, 1979

Table of Contents

Preface iii

PART ONE
Death in Other Cultures   **1**

1. Death and Ancient Finnish Culture
    Kalle Achté 3

2. Death and Society Among The Anggor of New Guinea
    Peter S. Huber 14

3. Religious Symbolism in Limbu Death-By-Violence
    Rex L. Jones 25

4. Freud, Durkheim, and Death Among the Sebei
    Walter Goldschmidt 34

5. The Good Death in Kaliai: Preparation for Death in
    Western New Britain
    David R. Counts 39

PART TWO
Death in The United States and Mexico   **45**

6. Death Shall Have No Dominion: The Passing of the
    World of the Dead in America
    Charles O. Jackson 47

7. The Days of the Dead in Oaxaca, Mexico:
    An Historical Inquiry
    Judith Strupp Green 56

8. The Death Culture of Mexico and Mexican Americans
    Joan Moore 72

9. The Black Experience with Death: A Brief Analysis
    through Black Writings
    Maurice Jackson 92

10. Death, Funeral and Bereavement Practices in
Appalachian and Non-Appalachian Kentucky
Thomas F. Garrity and James Wyss 99

PART THREE
War and Disaster   119

11. Death of Young Sons and Husbands
Lea Barinbaum 121

12. Grief Work and Dirty Work: The Aftermath of an Aircrash
Vanderlyn R. Pine 126

13. The Handling of the Dead in a Disaster
Marvin R. Hershiser and E. L. Quarantelli 132

14. Justifying the Final Solution
Helge Hilding Mansson 145

PART 1
Death
in
Other
Cultures

The causes of death and the meaning of death in other societies are often very different from our own. When these societies are isolated communities, lacking in modern technology, and applying strange-appearing words for unfamiliar concepts, we tend to view them as cute or quaint, sometimes attributing to them wisdom that may or may not be there, sometimes assuming that their beliefs are second best to our own.

An important purpose in learning about death in other societies is to place our own death beliefs in better perspective. For example, since many of the world's societies see sorcery or hostile external agents as the cause of most deaths, what does it imply for our society that the causes of death are usually viewed as coming from within the body? One possible response is that we may see the dying individual as responsible for his or her own death, rather than seeing death as the responsibility of others or of magic. Thus, if you are dying, it is because you did something to cause your own death, such as having poor health or dietary practices. This view is emphasized by some contemporary western social movements that claim that the individual is responsible for everything that happens to him or her. While this position may be a welcome antidote to the helpless feeling that all illness is caused by external agents, it has the additional effect of producing guilt about dying in the persons who are dying. It may also cause their friends and family—and even health professionals—to blame the dying person for the eventual death.

We can also see that most societies offer an active role to dead persons, often viewing them as potential enemies that require propitiation, or as potential guardians and supporters. They honor their dead to appease their dead. But we also honor our dead. Why? Is this a carry-over from the time when we also wanted to appease our dead? We tend to say that our ceremonies for the dead are really to help the living, and in the following chapters you will see an example of that also, but we still retain some feelings that the dead will "know" that we are honoring them. "My father would have wanted it that way." "My wife would be pleased if she knew." What do these familiar statements imply, if not some sort of ambivalance about the ability of the dead to remain aware of what we, the still-living, are doing for them?

These articles also point out that death ceremonies and death beliefs are integral parts of a coherent and cohesive social structure and social belief system. As societies change, their death ceremonies and beliefs change. When technology provides airplanes, we fly some cremated remains out into the ocean and drop them from the airplane. When science describes the universe, we are less likely to think of the dead going "up to heaven," at least in the literal sense. When population density and public health combine to keep us from placing the dead in shallow graves, we develop other procedures. So our death ceremonies and beliefs arise just as much from our own societal circumstances as do those of other societies.

The articles in Part One also throw another kind of spotlight on our own society: the extent to which we look for explanations in human physiology and genetics. We tend to believe that death occurs because our genetic structure requires that people die and that human physiology responds to this requirement. That does not appear to be a universal requirement. It does, however, reflect our view of the immense significance of the biomedical sciences.

The anthropological literature is filled with descriptions of death rituals and with studies of the causes of death and of dying. It has been many years since Leo Simmons published his book on aging and death in what we then called "primitive society," but no one has yet attempted a subsequent integration of how societies around the world view dying and death (1). Such an attempt would be particularly useful today, especially if it were related to the psychological, sociological, and medical literature on dying and death.

I would like to make one more observation. Death is one event that occurs in every society everywhere in the world, perhaps in the universe. And every society has a way of explaining death, each one believing that its way is the right way. Yet, I believe the truth remains that death is one event that our scientists know no more about than the sorcerers in New Guinea. We may know more about how dying occurs, at least the biological aspects, but none of us knows what death is. And so death may be a particularly good topic to begin exploration of differences in societal values around the world.

1. Simmons, L. W. *The role of the aged in primitive society.* New Haven: Yale University Press, 1945.

CHAPTER 1

Death
and
Ancient Finnish Culture

Kalle Achté

Belief in the Immortality of the Soul

Immortality of the soul is the most essential concept of all religions. Freud has regarded religion as a means of denying the reality of death and he thought that only very few persons can unconsciously believe that death really implies an ultimate cessation of everything [1]. Archaeological excavations have disclosed evidence suggesting that man possibly in some way or other has conceived man's bodily and spiritual duality and cherished certain burial rites which may be interpreted as aspirations to summon the departed soul back into the body. The deceased were buried close by the fireplace of dwellings so that its heat would rewarm the cold corpse for the soul to re-enter into it. The deathly pale face of the deceased was chafed with dyestuff which symbolized life. According to an ancient Karelian belief, the soul which had departed from the body when a person was passing away could be seen after the burial flying as a butterfly or bird. Kemppinen reported that even as late as in the summer of 1965 he heard in Ilomantsi, the easternmost parish of Finland (post WW II), how people in a family took it for granted that it was the soul of a young child who had died in February which flew after the interment into the house in the shape of a small white butterfly and sat down

on the face of the brother whom the deceased sister had loved much [2].
Primitive man has conceived the soul of a living person as being capable of
moving about outside the body as an entirely separate and independent entity.
Then the thought comes readily into one's mind that even the departure of
the soul from the body at death does not signify that the soul itself would die
off. It has been believed that in the hour of death the soul does indeed
become detached from the body, it departs through the mouth and remains
floating in the air near the body. The eyes of the deceased had to be closed in
order that the dead man could not select the one who would follow him.
Worship of the dead performed at the grave implied above all worship of the
immortal soul. The belief that the soul and the body are intimately connected
with each other even after death is illustrated by the consideration that the
deceased could stand up and get going from the cadaver in consequence
whereof relatives kept vigil by the dead man's body throughout the night for
some nights just as though watching over him.

Fear of the Ghosts

In order to prevent the corpse from starting out, the Karelians used to sew
together the ends of the stockings put on the deceased, and similarly the
mittens put on the deceased were sewn together at the ends, too. It was
another custom to tie the corpse in the middle with a belt onto the cadaver
board. The same custom has prevailed also in the other Nordic countries. It
was often related that the dead had been seen going around in defective shape,
since it was thought that having been buried in the grave would leave at least
some marks in them. The deceased were seen going as processions of the
dead. The dead were one-armed, one-eyed or one-legged [2]. Roman sorcery
includes plenty of incantations which disclose or advise what should be done
if such a great number of dwellers in the halls of Death would embark in the
sleigh of the deceased that the horse could not haul it. Votyaks believed that
souls of dead people would be haunting around specifically when someone
lies a-dying since those relatives who have died earlier come for him to bring
him into the family grave. All this indicates how difficult it is for man to
understand the irreversibility of death. Votyaks and Mordvinians used to place
a small table by the deceased and lay pasties brought by the neighbors in
order to give a treat to the souls who came for the deceased. These pasties
were called "the ransom of the soul". According to traditional belief, ghosts
made their appearance just in that attire in which the body was clad when
buried. Ghosts were of small size. It is very interesting to notice that ancient
Greek mythology has many features in common with ancient Finno-Ugric
mythology [3].

Personification of Death. Omens

Ever since the days of the primitive cave man, living people took care of the deceased on his way to the realm of death and of his life in the nether world by putting with the body into the grave utensils which he had needed when alive and which were believed to be indispensable for him in the life beyond. Belief in the resurrection of the body is another important element. The purpose of embalming was to promote the preservation of the body which was bound to be resurrected once again. In the Finnish national epic Kalevala [4] the poems about the hero Lemminkäinen relate how Lemminkäinen is raised from the dead. The belief in resurrection appearing in Finnish mythology concerning death involves a conviction that the body will become alive once again, and regain the soul and spirit [5]. In ancient mythical beliefs, death was personified in some way or other. It was lurking for human lives. Death could make its appearance as a night-time rider who sped by whizzlingly, or as some other appalling ghost or as the Man with the Scythe whose presence was best recognized by the one whom death had come for. Death has also been regarded as warm and associated with positive values. Furthermore, also illness was conceived as personified in ancient times. Omens could appear in dreams. Even today there are places where people believe that the dog senses if death is on the move in the neighborhood and expresses this by howling [6]. It is a very old belief that death is impending if a great black woodpecker, raven or some other bird of the woods perches on a tree growing in the yard. It was considered that a spotted woodpecker pecking at the wall of the house signifies nailing up of a coffin and heralds a death bound to occur soon in that house. Likewise, a cuckoo and black raven were birds of death, too. Not only death but also illnesses were personified. Illnesses were regarded as living beings. In Karelia there was an old custom that a person who was ill at the point of death was lifted off from his sickbed and laid down on the floor to pass away. According to Karelian belief, the one who was at the point of death, though apparently still alive in a state of lethargy, had a brother from the house of death already waiting for him to carry him away [7].

Bidding Farewell to the Dying Person and Reconciliation with Him

Within the Karelian cultural sphere it was an old established custom that prior to a person's imminent death, and immediately after it, people always went to him to bid him farewell and at the same time to make up mutually their differences and offenses. The person who was bound to die was taken by the hand, which also indicated parting. If, in spite of such actions, the surviving adversary did not get relieved of his anxiety and his guilt feelings did not disappear, he had still to pay a visit to the grave. When the patient was in a very bad condition, some elderly relative had to watch through the night by his bed. When the patient entered the dying stage, the watching relative had to wake up the people in the house to witness him to pass away, since it was an ill-starred circumstance if death occurred without anybody seeing it. After the patient had died, nobody in the house was allowed to sleep any more that night. The deceased felt relieved if he was not left alone after he had passed away. The suicide died suddenly, and thus people did not have time to make peace with him. This is why the suicides were dreaded after their death.

Customs Associated with Death and Burials

The corpse was washed as soon as possible and dressed immediately thereafter. The corpse of a suicide, lunatic or epileptic was not washed but was buried, lying prone on his stomach, in those clothes he had worn when he died. Such a corpse was lifted into the coffin with pokers, never with one's hands, so that the illness would not catch and remain running in the family. One had to be very careful not to put any metal objects nor garments containing metal into the coffin, since according to ancient Finnish ideas, metal burned like sparks when the deceased was crossing the river of Hades. In Karelia a bottle of spirits was put under the pillow when the corpse was laid down in the coffin. The deceased was provided with various implements which he might need during his journey to the house of death. These necessities included money which was put either in the mouth of the deceased or in the coffin. He needed the money to pay the ferryman on the river of Hades or to purchase his future abode in the realm of death. A similar custom prevailed among ancient Teutons. One was not allowed to look at the funeral procession through a window. In many countries the windows of the house were covered with shutters in order that the onlookers themselves would not die. By the gate of the home of the deceased, the horse hauling the coffin was pulled up once again so that the deceased could cast his last look at this earthly home of his which he now had to leave. The funeral procession made stops at nearby houses and crossroads, the intention of which was to drive death away and at the same time to give prominence to the solemnities. Before entering to the graveyard, the Karelian funeral procession stopped by a lopped-off memorial tree. In case that the soul of the deceased might perhaps attempt to return back to his old home, a ritual ceremony was performed during the journey before the gates of the graveyard. The ceremony involved partaking offerings, lopping branches off a tree and then carving the mark of the deceased on the lopped-off tree. Figure 1 represents such a mark carved on a memorial tree. The mourners also drank spirits by the tree. The function of the lopped-off memorial trees was to prevent the deceased from returning home. It has been claimed that huge tombstones would serve the same

Figure 1. A lopped-off memorial tree with marks of two deceased persons and the dates of their death carved on the trunk; from the parish of Pielisjärvi in Northern Karelia. Photographed by A. Laatikainen in 1928. By courtesy of Finnish Museum Bureau.

purpose, to hinder the deceased from escaping from his grave to go haunting. It may be inferred that behind the fear of ghosts there have been guilt feelings of the survivors for their hostile emotions towards the deceased. These guilt feelings were transferred into the spirit of the deceased which consequently would go haunting. If the survivors had purely positive feelings towards the deceased, any fears of him would hardly arise. Fear of the deceased is largely a reflection of one's own feelings of guilt.

In ancient Finnish culture there was a custom that after the final ceremonies had been conducted by the grave, the mourners once again took a look at the deceased so that he would get more air in his coffin. The participants in the funeral procession were treated to spirits and also the deceased was provided with liquor in the grave. A memorial meal was then eaten by the grave. Figures 2 and 3 represent mourners in a burial ceremony in eastern Karelia in the 1920s.

In this connection we quote an excerpt from a letter which V. Svaetichin wrote on September 17, 1929, from the village of Säiniö, then a village in a rural parish outside the city of Viipuri (Viborg) [8] :

Figure 2. The graveyard in the village of Varpakylä, in the parish of Suojärvi, the easternmost Karelian parish in Finland before WW II. The burial of Pelagea Kononen (née Koivunen). In the front row the daughters of the deceased are squatting, from the left Outi, Irinja and Fedosa. The bearded man in the back row is the husband of the deceased, Rodion Kononen (whose burial, again, is seen in Figure 3). In the middle crying and leaning on each other are Mrs. Tikkunen to the left and the youngest daughter of the deceased, Katri Kononen. On top of the grave, the board marked with a cross is the cadaver board. Photographed approximately in 1920 or 1921. The original photograph is in private collection. By courtesy of Finnish Museum Bureau.

In the village of Säiniö, in the rural parish of Viipuri, there is a Cross Pine (lopped-off memorial tree) of which I would like to mention the following things. This pine grows by the road leading to Kuolemajärvi, about 600 yards from the railway station of Säiniö (see Figure 4). In the trunk of this tree there are still seven wooden plates. In one wooden plate a cross mark is still very clearly visible, in another one a cross mark painted red can be seen, and in one plate placed lower in the tree

Figure 3. The graveyard in the village of Varpakylä. The burial of Rodion Kononen. The son of the deceased, Feodor Kononen, is seen in the front. In the middle there is a sack full of bread. Each guest in the funeral brought a bread as a gift. The breads were all gathered into the sack, and later after the burial the breads were distributed to the poor. To the far right there is a group waiting for the distribution of the breads; the group includes among others one gipsy. Photographed in about 1925. The original photograph is in private collection. By courtesy of Finnish Museum Bureau.

trunk several cross marks are discernible. The circumferential measure of the Cross Pine at its base is 9 ft. 8 in. It may be more than 200 years old. In the second photograph (Figure 5) I have marked seven arrows to indicate the places in the trunk where the wooden plates have been put. Earlier there have been much more of these wooden plates in the pine, but boys of the village have thrown stones on them so that many have fallen down.

People tell about these wooden plates that on the way to the burial site the funeral procession stopped by the Cross Pine and a small wooden plate was nailed up onto the trunk of the tree. On the plate a cross mark and the year of death of the deceased had been carved. If the deceased was an adult, the coffin was usually painted black; a dead boy's coffin was painted blue while the color of the coffin of a girl was red. Wooden plates were painted with respective colors. The relatives of the deceased treated to spirits, the bottle circulated from hand to hand. Finally a hymn was sung, and then the funeral procession started again

Figure 4. Cross Pine or a lopped-off memorial tree in the village of Säiniö, in the rural parish outside the city of Viipuri (Viborg). The lower branches of the pine have been lopped off in connection with several funeral ceremonies. Photographed by V. Svaetichin. By courtesy of Finnish Museum Bureau.

on its way to the graveyard. This memorial tree awed children and women so much that they did not dare to pass it in the dark. It is about half a century ago that such funeral ceremonies were conducted the last time. There is a similar Cross Pine near the church of Lemi which the local people call, by the name School Pine. I have not been able to find out why such a name has been given to that memorial tree. There is another Cross Pine in the rural parish of Viipuri, namely in the village of Ylivesi, this pine standing by the road which leads to Juustila. In all these other places the funeral ceremonies were almost similar.

A domestic animal was often slaughtered, a practice which suggests a sacrificial meal. According to Kemppinen [2], there was a custom that on returning

Figure 5. A detail of the Cross Pine in Figure 4. The seven arrows point to the wooden plates nailed up onto the trunk of the pine as a part of funeral ceremonies. Some of the arrows which are against the trunk are somewhat difficult to discern. Photographed by A. Svaetichin. By courtesy of Finnish Museum Bureau.

from the grave people whisked and beat each other on the back with twigs of silver fir and juniper, murmuring all the time: "Go home, don't stay here". On their way back the mourners endeavored through various ceremonies to make sure that the deceased and other ghosts could not come along with them but would remain in the graveyard. People were afraid of the deceased and his revenge. Therefore it was of utmost importance to worship the deceased with sufficient respect. Dead people were allowed to visit their old earthly home on only one particular day, the day of the deceased. This particular day in November is nowadays called All Saints' Day.

The sun sets in the west. Influenced by Sumerian and Egyptian beliefs, the Greeks assumed that the realm of death lies in the west.

According to ancient Finnish mythology, again, the realm of death was located in the north. Likewise the seat of all illnesses was in the north. Diseases were driven back there by sorcery.

The Projection of One's Own Feelings Into the Outer World as Demons

Sorcerers had several different names, one of them being "kade", which in the Finnish language is a direct derivative from the word meaning envy. This last-mentioned connection reflects in one way the background of ancient Finnish culture and, more generally, incantations practiced by man. One's own hostile and envious feelings are projected into the external world, which then is experienced as envious and malevolent and which consequently must be appeased. The opponents of the Finn were envious sorcerers and demons. Envious sorcerers were hostile fellow creatures, "people of the misfortune", who mobilized malicious powers. Incantations include endless descriptions about the deeds of envious sorcerers. The envious sorcerer could bring about misfortune by a mere glance. Here we encounter even in ancient Finnish culture the very primitive theme of the evil eye, which occurs in many different cultural spheres. It resembles the beliefs concerning witchcraft. Importune and troublesome people were driven away with embers. Fire was sacred and purifying.

Discussion

Belief in the immortality of the soul seems to be common to all religions and to the mythologies of various cultures. Freud has stressed that very few people can unconsciously realize the finality of death [1]. The present paper has considered various notions of immortality and various views of death, and events and omens associated with death in the light of ancient Finnish and Karelian (Karelia = a part of eastern Finland) religion and mythology, paying attention to certain attempted psychodynamic explanations.

It was typical of the ancient Finns to assume that the soul did not immediately leave the room where the deceased was lying but only a few days afterwards. Therefore it was important to say of the deceased nothing but good and perhaps to open some opening in the wall so that his soul could get out. A central position among the survivors' fears related to death was the fear of haunting. This is perhaps why the use of very big and heavy tombstones has been general in various cultural spheres. In Karelian culture the deceased was often tied up with the coffin, so as to prevent him from going haunting. It was important to make peace with the dying before his death, so that he would not afterwards do evil to others. The death of a suicide was therefore particularly dangerous, as he had not had time to make peace with other people before his unexpected and sudden death and was in consequence likely to haunt them later. Here we see people's inclination to project their own hostile and perhaps guilt-evoking thoughts onto the deceased, and be then afraid of his revenge.

Typical of the Karelian belief was that people who believed they had seen ghosts of dead persons described these as one-eyed, crippled and destroyed, or castrated as it were. A further reason for the fear of the deceased may have been that there was the danger of becoming similar to him. People believed that various omens had been seen prior to a death or suicide, such as an unknown black bird flying onto the yard of the house of the dying person, or a savage dog or cock. There was a tendency towards personifying the death just as illness.

One interesting old custom associated with death and funerals was the dedication to the deceased of a particular memorial tree. The deceased was mourned visibly, and in order to propitiate him, various gifts, either alcoholic drinks or food, were placed on the root of the tree or alcohol was consumed there, together with the deceased as it were, so as to prevent him getting angry. All this reflects the survivors' guilt and the projection of their own feelings onto the deceased.

All illustrations in this paper are published with permission of Museovirasto (Finnish Museum Bureau).

REFERENCES

1. S. Freud, Our Attitudes Towards Death, *Collected Papers of S. Freud*, Standard Edition XIV, Hogarth Press, London, 1962.
2. I. Kemppinen, Haudantakainen Elämä (Life Beyond the Grave), *Karjalan Tutkimusseura*, Helsinki, 1967.
3. U. Harva, *Altain Suvun Uskonto (Beliefs of the Altaic Tribe)*, WSOY, Porvoo, 1933.
4. *Kalevala*, English translation by W. F. Kirby, Everyman's Library, London, 1966.
5. M. Haavio, *Suomalainen Mytologia (Finnish Mythology)*, WSOY, Porvoo, 1967.
6. K. A. Achté and J. Lönnqvist, Death and Suicide in Finnish Mythology and Folklore, *Psychiatria Fennica*, *3*, pp. 59-63, 1972.
7. S. Paulaharju, *Syntymä, Lapsuus ja Kuolema (Birth, Childhood and Death)*, WSOY, Porvoo, 1924.
8. V. Svaetichin, Written communication, 1929.

CHAPTER
2

Death and Society Among The Anggor of New Guinea[1,2]

Peter S. Huber

Concern with the social meaning of death is in no way a novel preoccupation for a social anthropologist. During the early decades of the 20th century, Hertz (1960), Rivers (1926) and Van Gennep (1960) each attempted to formulate generalizations about the mortuary practices and eschatological doctrines encountered in primitive society. In so doing, they designated "death" as a universal cultural category, and therefore an important and distinctive topic for anthropological scrutiny. Though each was writing independently, all three authors drew attention to the transitional aspect of death, in both doctrine and rite. That is, from the perspective of any community or society, the death of any person involves both a radical change in the nature of the social relationship between deceased and survivors and a redefinition of the surviving community as well. For example, the deceased may become an ancestor rather than a kinsman and come to require special forms of propitiation or avoidance in his new status; similarly, the reallocation of statuses and roles, or the redefinition of group composition and intergroup relations may be required. In their diverse cultural forms, then, rites and beliefs associated with death relate both to change and renewal rather than termination.

[1] This paper is based on research sponsored by the U. S. Public Health Department under NIMH Grant T01 MH-1229 and NIMH Fellowship F-1-MH 45391. This paper is a revision of an earlier paper presented under the same title in a session on War and Peace in Primitive Society at the American Anthropological Association Meetings in New York, November, 1971. Nancy Bowers, James Fox, J. Christopher Crocker, and particularly Richard Huntington were kind enough to read the initial draft and offer a number of helpful suggestions, many of which have been incorporated into the final copy.
[2] Research for this paper took place from November, 1969 to March, 1971 in the severe terrain of the West Sepik District, New Guinea. The Anggor speakers number approximately 1000 and are distributed among twelve villages varying between twelve and 170 persons in size. The Anggor practice a mixed form of subsistence which includes horticulture, sago cultivation and hunting and gathering. Fieldwork was conducted mainly at the Wamu village, from which approximately one-half of the total Anggor populace could be surveyed. Case history material referred to in this paper was elicited by inquiring into the cause and manner of death of deceased persons encountered in geneaology, and by leading older informants into narratives and discussions of their personal experiences with sorcery, ambush, raid and warfare.

However, there is another point in the work of Rivers, Hertz, and Van Gennep—implicit rather than clearly stated—which is more relevant to the ensuing discussion of death in Anggor society. That is, that many of the symbols and concepts relating to mortuary practice and eschatological belief must be multi-referential and serve to relate the natural phenomenon of biological death to more basic, abstract features of the social system. Rivers, for example, argues that in "primitive belief" the process of death transforms persons from one arbitrary, culturally defined status and role to another; therefore the full cultural meaning of death cannot be understood in purely biological or even psychological terms, but only in relation to general ideas about social order which involve categorical distinctions and complementarities between the social statuses of living and dead persons. If death is to be regarded as a social transition, then clearly it cannot be understood without reference to the broader framework of the social system which defines the termini of the process. Conversely, a clearer understanding of the conceptual scheme of the social system may be obtained through familiarity with the ways in which death, in a given cultural context, is considered to effect social transition.

Hertz, for example, continually alludes to the process of decomposition referred to as the separation of flesh and bone as the key element in mortuary practices involving secondary burial. In all of his discussion he treats this separation as a natural rhythm, obviously well suited to serve as analogue or metaphor for the social transition of death. Yet recent work by Leach (1966) and Levi-Strauss (1969) indicate that flesh and bone are also widely encountered as natural idioms of social relationship and differentiation. For example, in the procreation belief of various societies it is held that an individual receives bone (male substance) from his father, and flesh (female substance) from his mother, and that his connection with his mother's people can be regarded as one of flesh, his connection with his agnates as one of bone. It seems reasonable to suggest that in such societies the image of decomposition, the separation of bone and flesh, may symbolize more than a simple change in the social status of the deceased. It may, for example, signify the dissolution of a connection between discrete and autonomous groups, temporarily joined by their complementary procreative contributions to the person of the deceased—and therefore constitute a redefinition and purification of the groups involved. The point here is that primitive rites and beliefs relating to death cannot be regarded as purely superstitious responses to a biological phenomenon, but as expressing certain critical aspects of social order and its continuity.

Although this chapter is not concerned with the transitional aspects of death, nor with physiological images of the social system, it does involve the more general problem of the relationship between conceptions of death and conceptions of social order—in this case, conceptions of community boundaries and relations with the outside world. The Anggor conceive of inter-community relationships primarily in terms of a substrate of perpetual hostility, occasionally erupting in conventional manifestations of homicide and warfare.

This conception is expressed through ideas about death, just as episodes of violence can be triggered by the actual occurrence of death. According to informants, raiding, treachery, and sorcery were common in pre-contact times, and in this former period men would not leave their villages without bow, arrows, and cane breast-plate, nor would they go far into the bush alone; also during this period, women engaged in domestic tasks outside the immediate vicinity of the village would be constantly guarded by men with weapons at hand. Although episodes of open violence have been substantially curtailed since the establishment of the Australian presence in the late 1950s, they still occur sporadically and the undercurrent of inter-village hostility is still a dominant feature of Anggor culture and daily life. One might be inclined to wrongly suppose that patterns of inter-village hostility and aggression can best be understood as a series of revenge transactions between groups; but, in fact, the key to inter-village relationships is the structural autonomy and "moral isolation" of the local community. This involves a "we/they"—"member/outsider" dichotomy represented mainly in Anggor beliefs about the nature of the relationship between the individual and his community, and the manner in which this relationship is transmogrified through death—by definition the result of hostile action by outsiders. That is, constant hostility is maintained and episodic violence generated by the fact that virtually every Anggor death represents an attack by one community upon another. Consequently, the ensuing paper will consider first the Anggor beliefs about death and sorcery and their relationship to village definition, and then to the ways in which violent episodes erupt within this framework.

ALIENATION OF THE "VITAL SPIRIT"

Surely for many societies there is a sense in which one can regard the killing of a village member by an outsider as an attack upon the community: indeed the proposition seems almost tautological. Yet for the Anggor the death of any person represents more than a loss of population. Very specific notions of metaphysical loss and danger to the community are implicit in the Anggor concept of death. And by definition death can only result from the active aggression of specific individuals.

Above all else, Anggor informants represent death as the final separation of the two vital metaphysical components of the person: *ifiaf* ("vital spirit") and *hohoanum* ("consciousness" or "personality"). In life "vital spirit" is completely subordinated to "consciousness": a consciousness which is in part rational and socially shared, deriving from the internalization of social categories and principles of village organization. Thus the living person represents a subordination of the undirected vital energy of the *ifiaf* to the collective consciousness of the community. This subordination is ritually expressed through regular episodes of spirit possession in which the individual consciousness is "covered" (Pidgin: *karimapim*)—obscured and superceded—by that of the *sanind*, guardian spirits, who function both to protect the community against external threats and to maintain internal order and harmony. In death, the personal consciousness, the *hohoanum*, ceases to exist and the *ifiaf* is liberated from its directions; its transformed presence constituting a serious, if transient, threat to the community. The powers of the liberated *ifiaf* are potentially great, and the more frightening because they are beyond social or rational influence—one cannot relate to the capricious spirits of the dead, one can only avoid them. Yet the danger of the liberated *ifiaf* is also mitigated by this same capriciousness, for without rational consciousness the *ifiaf* cannot effectively focus its awesome powers—which begin to dissipate shortly after death. Thus Anggor mortuary practice is not concerned with social transition but with the isolation and banishing of the spirits of the deceased. After a night-long vigil over the remains of the deceased, they are buried with little ceremony in a garden far from the main village. In the nights that follow, doors are ritually sealed at sundown against the passage of the liberated *ifiaf* which may assume a spectral form and walk abroad. The *sanind*, guardian spirits, which aided and possessed a man in life will congregate at his grave to mourn his death—but also to protect the surviving community from the malicious aims of his *ifiaf*. Thus, any death diminishes the capital of vital force under the control of community by alienating a portion of it and endangers the community by transforming that portion into a powerful and menacing presence.

SORCERY AND DEATH

This alienation of *ifiaf* from consciousness, and so from community, can ideally result only from the direct, physical, and conscious sorcery of "outsiders". Sorcery requires a physical attack upon the person of the victim, employing conventional weapons which have been ritually treated with powerful spells and herbs. The treatments convey both invincibility and invisibility, so that the victim may be taken unawares and killed instantly and secretly. The victim is then healed of wounds, resurrected and returned to his village as though nothing had happened, remembering nothing of the episode. Yet he has been "programmed" to die at a certain time of some specific apparent cause, and subsequently does so. When this happens, his co-villagers realize that the deceased has been the victim of sorcery—though the details of the episode remain shrouded in secrecy and can be revealed only through a process of divination. Whether there are, in fact, individuals who engage in such practices is a question for which no direct evidence is available; surely this must seem unlikely to the western observer. Yet there are eyewitness accounts of sorcery incidents, and persons who indirectly allow or even encourage others to regard them as sorcerers to no apparent political advantage. The point is that Anggor definitions of village boundaries and inter-village hostilities are predicated upon beliefs about sorcery and the system operates as if sorcerers existed.

When queried in general terms, Anggor informants state categorically that disease, accident, and even homicide are merely apparent or proximate causes of death: that sorcery (*asunind*) is at the base of all terminal afflictions. Although the Anggor frequently engage in elaborate ceremonies aimed at curing various specific illnesses, informants allege that illness is treated because it is unpleasant and debilitating, but does not constitute a direct threat to life itself. More important, when questioned as to the cause or manner of death of a specific person encountered in geneaology, informants rarely make reference to physical symptoms of disease (unless bizarre) or to native categories of affliction. Of 177 case histories of death collected in this fashion for four different villages, 128 or 72 percent were attributed unequivocally to sorcery. Another 23 were attributed to miscellaneous causes including introduced epidemics, extraordinary intervention of spirits, and old age—the last of which can be regarded, for reasons I shall not enumerate, as involving a special form of sorcery. The remaining 26 (15 percent) were attributed to homicide. In theory homicide results from sorcery, like any other form of death: informants argue, for example, that arrow wounds cannot be fatal unless their victim has been previously attacked by a sorcerer and programmed to die by such wounds. In at least three of the 26 cases referred to here, deaths from homicide were ultimately laid at the door of a known, third-party sorcerer. Regardless of whether homicides are ultimately responsible for the deaths of their victims in any given instance, attempts to commit murder in the conventional fashion are distinctly a part of the pattern of inter-village hostility among the Anggor and will be discussed in the context of episodes of overt violence. The present point is that the relentless natural phenomenon of death is so conceived by the Anggor that it provides a perfect symbol of the relentless underlying enmity which obtains between villages.

Just as the Anggor automatically presume that any death is the result of sorcery, they presume that any unknown sorcerer operating against their village is an outsider. Of 128 deaths attributed to sorcery, the sorcerer was named in 101 (79 percent), and in 98 of these 101, he was said to be of a different village than his victim. In the 27 cases in which the identity of the sorcerer was not specifically known, informants presumed that he was a member of an alien village—though no speculation as to the identity of the sorcerer or his village was ever offered. The identity of sorcerers is not deduced from specific, known sources of special enmity—i.e., quarrels or conflicts— but the general presumption of guilt against all alien villages is converted into specific and certain knowledge of complicity through a process of public divination. Since the *ifiafs* of recently deceased men invariably pay repeated visits to the homes of the sorcerers who have liberated them, the divination process is exceedingly simple. Men of the victim's village maintain a nightly vigil for several days after burial, waiting for the *ifiaf* to reveal the sorcerer. On its nocturnal perambulations the *ifiaf* assumes the form of an intense white light visible for miles, so that it is easy for watchers—including casual observers from other villages—to identify the guilty village and subsequently the individual culprit. In addition to revealing the identity of the sorcerer, the *ifiaf* visits the site of the original attack and enables watchers from the victim's village to reconstruct the entire episode. Thus a chain of events is made visible which were originally covert and cloaked in secrecy—an end which is greatly valued in its own right.

In fact, identifying the source of aggression is more important as a public response to sorcery than is actual revenge. Although, as indicated, informants could name sorcerers in 101 out of 128 sorcery deaths, they could identify acts of retribution—revenge killing—in only 30 of the cases. Of these 30 vengeance killings only 19 were executed by the village of the sorcerer's victim: 12 against the sorcerer himself, 3 against persons of the sorcerer's village, and 4 against unrelated and presumably innocent third parties who had the misfortune to be readily accessible. The remaining 11 cases of vengeance killing cited by informants were mainly coincidental killings of sorcerers by members of third party villages, acting on motives of their own. Although informants consider direct reciprocity—the reciprocal killing of a sorcerer by the co-villagers of his victim—an especially satisfactory form of revenge, the variations indicated above are all regarded as perfectly acceptable alternatives. If a sorcerer from village A kills a man of village B and is subsequently murdered by village C in connection with some other quarrel, village B considers itself satisfactorily avenged. Or, satisfactory revenge for sorcery may be obtained through the murder of some convenient and apparently innocent third party, related to the sorcerer either marginally or not at all. For example, the widow of a sorcery victim—if she is originally from a distant village and has no brothers at hand to protect or avenge her—is not infrequently made the object of revenge for her husband's death. Thus, informants' constant and earnest assertions that they avenge the deaths of all village mates must not be taken at face value. Clearly deaths are rarely exchanged between villages on a *quid pro quo* basis. Such statements have a structural significance, relating to the way in which society is ordered overall rather than to the actions that individuals should or do take in certain specified circumstances.

Anggor assertions about the taking of revenge are very similar to Anggor postulations of sister-exchange as the ideal form of marriage. That is, in discussing the institution of marriage in general, Anggor informants invariably observe that men should obtain wives by exchanging their sisters; more generally they may characterize the relationship between two exogamous groups as one based upon the reciprocal exchange of sisters. Yet if one examines individual marriage histories, one discovers that the direct exchange of one woman for another, either between men or between groups, is extremely rare. The fact is that women are bestowed gratis upon any man not of their own exogamous group—an act which simultaneously fulfills and creates an outstanding debt. Since women are rarely given specifically in return for other specific women, debts can never be clearly and finally cancelled, but are vaguely cumulative. Thus the relationship between exogamous groups is defined as one of indebtedness, and the bestowal of any woman defined as one link in a chain of unspecified exchanges. So it is with sorcery and death. Since direct reciprocity is not necessary for revenge—indeed, revenge itself, in the conventional sense, is not strictly necessary—deaths in different villages need not be directly linked. Hostile relations between villages are defined in terms of a backlog of unavenged deaths—and any given death is by definition simply one further evidence of this hostility, one more element in a hypothetical series of unspecified aggressions. Seen from this perspective, the taking of revenge through the slaying of apparently innocent third parties is perfectly logical; for third parties are, by definition, never innocent.

The preceding discussion of Anggor beliefs relating to sorcery, eschatology, and the relation of person to community—admittedly sketchy—demonstrates the manner in which the biological fact of death is utilized as a central element in the symbolic representation of village definition and inter-village relations. The remainder of the paper, then, will be concerned with the translation of this symbolic representation into social action; that is, with the way in which the ideal of hostility generates episodes of violence, again focusing on individual facts of biological death.

OVERT AGGRESSION

A necessary preliminary consideration is the relationship between covert acts of sorcery—discussed in the previous section—and overt acts of aggression—the main topic of the present section. It has been observed that in Anggor theory all deaths are ultimately due to sorcery, and further that overt acts of aggression can normally succeed in killing only those persons who have already been attacked by sorcery. Thus one might infer that overt aggression is ancillary to sorcery: that aggressors are mere tools, manipulated by sorcerers, with neither initiative nor responsibility. Anggor informants, however, flatly deny this. Some attempt to equivocate by suggesting that it is actually theoretically possible but exceedingly difficult to cause death through overt aggression alone: but this argument is generally regarded as moot—one could never be certain that a given homicide was not the result of sorcery—and irrelevant. For most informants the critical point is that, regardless of the conditions of its success, an attempt at homicide through overt aggression is a conscious, deliberate act in which one assumes responsibility for death through an immediate rather than final cause. The significance of this responsibility is evident in the fact that in those homicide case histories involving overt attacks in which the death was ultimately attributed to a known third party sorcerer, revenge was directed against the overt assailant, the immediate cause, rather than the sorcerer. Conversely, if a sorcerer of village A causes the death of a man of village B, and the villagers of B subsequently ambush the sorcerer and kill him openly, without the use of occult techniques, both villages regard the transaction as an equivalent exchange— in spite of the argument that the sorcerer had ultimately been killed by some other, unspecified sorcerer, unrelated to either village. Thus, in practice, acts of sorcery and acts of overt, non-magical aggression are equivalent and inter-changeable manoeuvres in the patterns of lethal exchange which characterize regular inter-village relations.

In consonance with the representation of inter-village relations discussed in the preceding section, face–to–face relations between persons of different villages are not frequent, but regular, amicable and wary. They may become temporarily strained through knowledge or suspicion of attacks by members of one village upon members of the other, but serious—if temporary—rupture of normal social relations generally results only from intense, overt forms of aggression such as ambush or raid. The question, then, is how are extraordinary episodes of massive aggression generated within the constant give and take of death which characterizes the normal condition of veiled hostility? The answer lies in certain fortuitous conjunctions of motive and means.

In considering the question of motive, it is essential to realize that acts of aggression or violence cannot properly be regarded as elements of broader political/economic strategies. As preceding observations on revenge and reciprocity indicate, there is no context in which violent attacks are required in the fulfillment of social obligations. Moreover, neither persons nor groups can gain material or symbolic advancement through violence. No case histories have been discovered in which land, women or goods have changed hands as a result of homicide or warfare—even in episodes which rendered the victims totally helpless. Nor are known sorcerers or homicides accorded any special prestige, aside from a judicious deference and avoidance: often they are regarded with ambivalence and may become isolated from their kinsmen. For although the killing of alien villagers is considered right and proper in the abstract, in practice it exposes one's friends and kinsmen to the threat of retaliation. Thus a notoriously successful sorcerer may so endanger his co-villagers that they determine to kill him themselves in the interest of their own safety. The point is that acts of violence among the Anggor cannot be regarded as instrumentalities, and the motives which underlie them cannot be apprehended as ends to which violence constitutes a means.

Instead, violence is expressive—both of the nature of the system and of contingent, temporary, individual states of being. Although Anggor informants find queries about motivation basically pointless, they generally respond on both of these levels: i.e. "A killed B because B was a stranger (or from a village which previously killed one of A's kinsmen)", or "A killed B because A was in a furious rage (or simply happened to feel like killing someone)". Observations such as the latter, relating to personal states of being, may be casually offered when they are obvious, but informants do not consider them to be essential to motivation, or even very illuminating. It is an essential feature of the Anggor view of man that individual processes of consciousness and motivation are largely non-rational, idiosyncratic, and unpredictable. Motives are not classified or imbued with ethical significance. The fact that A kills B can be taken as a clear indication that A wanted to kill B, and that bald statement of desire is all that another person can know with certainty about A's state of consciousness, or needs to know. As long as A's victim is a member of another village, the act is ethically sound, and beyond that cannot even be judged as wise or foolish—for even if the act leads to further unpleasant consequences, no one can say whether A's desire to kill B was sufficiently intense to justify the consequences.

As an outsider, one can go a step beyond this nihilistic individualism and characterize the situation in terms of a continuum of motive, with "intense anger" and "whimsey" (or "residual anger") as its poles. This suggests a general connection between anger and violence which is, in fact, encountered in symbolic and linguistic usages relating to the concept of "heat". The Anggor word for "anger" can be glossed as "internal heat"; on the other hand, acts of overt or covert violence and their associated paraphenalia are often described by informants as "hot". This general quality of heat is best exemplified when men react to the death of a close friend or kinsman by seizing their weapons and storming into the jungle, killing either the man responsible for the death or, by proxy, any other available outsider—in such a case, the killing generates the heat of anger, which generates the heat of further killing. On the other hand, the heat of anger arising from causes less compelling than the death of a kinsman may also lead to killing. Thus, in conflict over women or land, men occasionally resort to violence not as a means of resolving the quarrel, but as an expression of anger generated by it. In one case history, an extended state of inter-village war stemmed from a killing which in turn had resulted from a fit of rage brought on by a fortuitous series of annoying accidents as trivial as falling in the mud. Ultimately it depends on circumstance, chiefly on access to suitable victims, whether the heat of anger finds expression in the heat of violence. Anger which is not expressed in violence may dissipate in time, possibly leaving a residue to serve as the motive of future violence. Such residual anger receives an indirect expression, eventuated by circumstance just as its direct expression was inhibited by circumstance. Thus, a defenseless stranger, encountered by chance in the bush, may be slain for no apparent reason. Informants often attribute such killings to whimsey, for in many cases they have no way of identifying the source of the residual anger or heat so expressed. Thus, for the Anggor, the basic motive behind violence is the emotional state of anger, the source and intensity of which reflect a wide range of personal considerations. It is essential to realize that the Anggor make no important distinction between rational and irrational motives, as the western observer is tempted to do, but regard such apparent differences as a function of imperfect states of knowledge on the part of observers.

In order to understand the kinds of circumstances which in conjunction with certain intensities of motivation may give rise to intense, overt violence, various technical difficulties associated with killing must be considered. Within their own system of beliefs, the Anggor are confronted with the dilemma that sorcery is effective but dangerous to the practitioner, while overt violence is safer but more difficult to succeed at. Although sorcery involves techniques which can be learned through careful tuition, real skill requires a special predilection and comes only to a few. Since the sorcerer normally uses invisibility and invincibility to seek his victim on the latter's home ground, thus exposing himself to alien sorcerers and alien bush spirits (i.e. the *sanind*, guardians, of other villages), exceptional skill is indispensible and those who lack it prudently eschew sorcery as a means of violence. On the other hand, the weapons available for overt, non-magical forms of violence—unbalanced and unfletched arrows and bone daggers—are notably inefficient. Thus, success in overt violence depends primarily upon a combination of surprise and superiority of numbers. The ability of individuals or small groups inflamed by the death of a villagemate to express their anger through homicide then depends upon their skill in sorcery or, failing that, upon a chance encounter with suitable victims. Ideal victims include unprotected alien women engaged in subsistence activities which take them far from their home villages, or alien men, hunting or fishing etc. alone or in pairs and far from the aid of their co-villagers. Such victims are also "sitting ducks" for sorcerers and, further, provide opportunities which those inclined to violence by residual anger may find difficult to pass up. These chance concatenations of means and motive, leading to sorcery or overt homicide, serve to maintain the regular give-and-take of inter-village hostility—and the deaths which result may serve to trigger the sporadic large scale episodes of violence which temporarily disrupt normal social relations.

The difference in degree between the more sensational, sporadic episodes of violence and the more "regular" forms of aggression relates to the fact that the former are widely and intensely shared throughout an entire village and focussed specifically on an alien community. Since community motivation is essentially a spontaneous summation and intensification of personal feelings—i.e. among the Anggor, at least—it is non-rational and unpredictable. Yet the numbers and the focus involved introduce special tactical considerations into the picture. Sorcery, which requires complete secrecy and limited groups, is unsuitable for mass participation: because of the specific focus of community anger, random scouting for victims is out of the question and careful premeditation essential. Consequently, violence takes the form of raid or ambush with the dual goals of surprise and radical superiority of numbers. The Anggor do not regard violence as a test of either skill or courage, but as an expression of anger, or "heat," through murder; thus treachery is frequently enlisted and numbers exaggerated through the addition of allies. Whether the aim is to ambush a specific individual or to rout an entire village, the occurrence of a battle—even with the most unfair odds—must be judged a tactical failure. For once actual fighting is joined, it is unlikely that any participant on either side will be killed. Given the nature of Anggor weapons, it is almost impossible to inflict a mortal wound without exposing oneself to similar misfortune. And that is a risk which the Anggor are frankly unprepared to assume.

These various considerations are well illustrated in the narrative of a battle involving four villages—three against one—which was the largest known to informants:

> The principal antagonists in the battle, precipitated by a treacherous murder, were *Mate* and *Amasura* villages. Yowos of Mate village had encountered a large hunting party from Amasura resting on Mate land, and had been invited to share food and conversation with them. While doing so, he was shot in the back by Moindan of Amasura (joined by others) who was inflamed by lust for Yowos' wife. Yowos' nephew, who had accompanied him, narrowly escaped with his life and fled back to Mate village with news of the treachery. The men of Mate seized their weapons and hurried to the site of attack, but Amasura had departed. Mate then sent word to two neighboring villages who joined forces with them the next morning for a raid on Amasura. The people of Amasura were gathered in their village and prepared for the attack, and successfully battled the superior force over a wide range of territory throughout the day. When the battle was finally broken off at sunset, neither side had suffered serious casualty and the allies returned directly to their home villages. Several days later parties from both villages met in the jungle at their common boundary and bitterly debated the killing and the possibility of compensation. In the end Amasura refused to offer compensation and Mate determined to let the matter rest. Normal social relations were gradually resumed and the incident closed.

Though the preceding case is a good illustration of a large scale episode of violence, it is "typical" only in certain respects, i.e., it was an attempt to express anger against Amasura village through murder, by obtaining the greatest possible advantage of surprise and numbers. Excepting the directed quality of violence, these characteristics are common to all acts of aggression, even those on a small scale. Other features of the episode—the enlistment of allies, the immediate response, the short duration—represent contingent tactical decisions. The men of Mate could equally have chosen to wait several days and attempt to surprise a lone Amasura family pursuing subsistence activities in the jungle, or to wait a much longer time, maintain normal relations, and ultimately lead one or more Amasura men into a treacherous ambush. Moreover, they could have chosen to pursue the issue through subsequent raids and battles. The decisions actually made can be regarded as a vector sum of collective sentiment (the intensity of feeling required a direct response but could not be sustained through a series of raids) and judgements about alternative tactics (the Amasura would have been extremely wary of ambush for some time following). A further contingency bearing upon the episode was the fact that no casualties were inflicted on Amasura which could stimulate counter-retaliation. The point here is that sporadic, large-scale episodes have no characteristic form of their own, aside from that common to all forms of aggression, but are shaped by the circumstances which generate them. Thus, there is no categorical distinction—either in ideology or in practice—between large and small scale Anggor violence. As the number of persons involved in acts of aggression increases, the episodes become increasingly directed, premeditated, and public, and more disruptive of normal inter-village relations.

DEATH AND THE SOCIAL ORDER

For the Anggor, then, the relationship between ideas about death and ideas about social order—as suggested in the introduction—can be found on several related but not strictly integrated levels of analysis. In the first place, beliefs about death as a natural phenomenon, ultimately caused by sorcery arising in the outside world, symbolically represent the structural autonomy of the village. That is, they depict a moral cosmology in which each separate community is to its members an island of harmony and order beset on all sides by danger and chaos. Such beliefs do not represent psychological displacement, in the sense that "outsiders" are used as scapegoats to explain death: death is natural and inevitable and used to represent or explain the difference between outsiders and co-villagers. Whereas beliefs about death serve to express structural or categorical distinctions, the ideal of reciprocal violence between villages derives from these distinctions and provides a transactional model of relationship. This transactional model occupies a level of significance which mediates between the "structural" meaning of death, and the role of death in the action frame of reference. It preserves the logical features of beliefs about death, but relates them to social practice in a way that allows for flexibility in coping with a wide range of contingencies. All acts of violence, then, on any scale, find their meaning in the ideal model of inter-village relation symbolized in sorcery and reciprocal killing, and take their impetus from the "heat" of anger generated by previous acts of violence leading to death. Clearly Anggor ideas about death and about inter-village relations are inextricably linked on every level.

REFERENCES

Hertz, Robert. *Death and The Right Hand* (trans. by Rodney and Claudia Needham). Glencoe, Illinois: The Free Press, 1960.

Leach, Edmund. *Rethinking Anthropology*. London: The Athlone Press, 1966 (rev. ed.).

Levi-Strauss, Claude. *The Elementary Structures of Kinship* (trans. by John Bell, John von Sturmer, and Rodney Needham). Boston: Beacon Press, 1969.

Rivers, W.H.R. *Psychology and Ethnology*. New York: Harcourt Brace & Co., 1926.

Van Gennep, Arnold. *The Rites of Passage* (trans. by Monika Vizedom and Gabrielle Caffee). Chicago: University of Chicago Press, 1960.

CHAPTER
3

Religious Symbolism
in Limbu
Death-By-Violence

Rex L. Jones

INTRODUCTION[1]

Religions display a tremendous variety of rituals and myths that deal with the destiny of the human soul, with the diagnosis of disease, and with curing and healing, all of which indicates a preoccupation with the dying and decaying human body. The rites of passage at birth, puberty, and death, which are almost universal in human society, may be viewed as attempts to symbolically order the natural process of a decaying universe embodied in the life cycle of a human being. Fertility cults, agricultural rituals, and hunting magic further display an attempt on the part of man to control the life and death process itself through a symbolic control of nature and a creation of order and purpose to existence. Even national and tribal rituals, or rituals of state, designed on the surface to further the political process such as coronations of royalty, independence day celebrations, world renewal ceremonies, or honorific rituals for important political figures and heroes are filled with the intent to symbolically create political and societal order. A survey of salvation movements, millenarian cults, or messianic dreams reveals an obsession on the part of men to bring order out of chaos and create a world free of disease, poverty, suffering, and death. Finally, religious ecstasy and mysticism, regardless of the sociological functions, display an attempt on the part of man to gain eternal life, free from death and the endless cycle of suffering and decay.

[1] A slightly different version of this paper was presented at the American Anthropological Association Meetings in New Orleans, 1973. The research on which this article is based was undertaken jointly with my wife, Shirley Kurz Jones, from October 1967 to January 1969 in eastern Nepal. Most of the data were gathered in the area near Terhathum Bazaar in the Terhathum administrative district. Thanks go to the Research Foundation of the State University of New York for a summer Grant-in-aid while preparing the manuscript for publication.

In the forefront of this obsession with order and decay stands the religious leader—the prophet, the shaman, the medicine man, and priest. The prophet through visions, dreams, and revelations encapsulizes and transmits to his followers a world of perfection, free from disease, poverty, suffering, and death. Through his charisma, this perfected universe becomes a living reality, attainable for the faithful and the true believer. The shaman and medicine man symbolize the same principle. In their initial illness through possession and the trance, they encounter illness, death, and destruction. Eventually, generally through an apprenticeship, they learn to control this chaotic state of the universe which is embodied in their own life. They soon learn to summon the spirit world at will and transform its supernatural power into a controlled secular power with which they manipulate the potentially destructive forces of the secular world. By controlled ecstasy they bring order to the lives of men. The priest, in a less dramatic fashion, accomplishes the same thing. Through ritual, prayer, and petition he summons divine order to a troubled world. The prophet, shaman, and priest merely represent "stages" of the religious process, ecologically adapted to the needs of men. In their role as religious leaders, they symbolize the longing for order and perfection in a disordered and imperfect world.

As an illustration of this principle, I propose to briefly examine concepts of death as expressed in a death ritual which I observed while doing fieldwork among a Tibeto-Burman speaking people of eastern Nepal, the Limbu. The ritual is not a normal death ritual, even by Limbu definitions, since it concerns an accidental, violent death, but it nevertheless makes clear much of the esoteric symbolism in normal Limbu funeral practices and reveals more clearly the uncertainty and hopelessness that death brings, and the Limbu's attempts to abolish it.

The Limbu of eastern Nepal number approximately 150,000 people. Today, they live in a multi-ethnic mountain community dominated politically and economically by caste Hindus, especially Brahmans and Chetris. This domination is relatively recent, having occurred in the last two centuries as a result of conquests by the Hindu monarchy of central Nepal. Large scale immigrations of caste Hindus and other ethnic groups followed the conquest, and today it is estimated that Limbus number less than twenty-five per cent of the population of their indigenous homeland, frequently referred to as Limbuan. Because of complex land tenure rights and relative political autonomy enjoyed in the nineteenth and twentieth century, Limbus have maintained a cultural and ethnic identity that differs considerably from their Hindu neighbors and conquerors. Although they have adopted a subsistence pattern based on wet rice agriculture that is almost indistinguishable from that of the Hindus in the area, they retain many features of the southeast Asian culture complex. This is especially evident in the distinctions made between normal deaths of old age and disease and abnormal deaths by accident or in childbirth.

Origins of Life and Death in Limbu Mythology

In Limbu mythology, God, *Porokmi Yambami* (Brahmā) created the first man (Tāpunāmā Wāhināmā) by mixing ashes and the droppings of chickens. He then breathed life into his creation and the man moved, but he could not talk. God took the tongue of a fish and made man's tongue so that he could speak. Thus, man is composed of the four basic elements of fire, earth, air, and water symbolized by ashes, dung, the breath of God, and the fish that live in water. The life principle identified with the breath of God, is indestructible, but one's corporeal existence is perishable and returns eventually to the basic elements. Originally, say the Limbu, God made a man of gold and silver, but he could not make him speak. Had God accomplished his task with his first creation, man would have eternal life, but for the price of speech, he pays with death. Death is, therefore, inevitable, but there are many ways of dying.

Thus, normal deaths of old age or disease are accepted as inevitable, as the work of God, or rather as a result of his failure to create a perfect man. Abnormal deaths by violence, accident, or in childbirth, are caused by the failures of men who are tempted by evil spirits. Out of envy and jealousy of the living, these spirits cause men to die prematurely. The spirits of men who die normally go to a land of the dead, after their bodies have been given a proper burial and they have been pacified with a period of mourning and a feast. The souls of men who die abnormally remain on earth, near their homes or places of death, to harass and plague the living, and out of jealousy and envy, they cause others to die in the same fashion.

The spirits of those who die by violence or accident (*soghā*), women who die in childbirth (*sugut*), and stillbirths (*susik*), originated in mythological times as a result of the desires and failures of men. One version of a myth tells how the first woman, *Tāpunāmā-Wāhināmā*, out of loneliness sought a child. She was impregnated by a storm and gave birth to a male child. On reaching weaning age, the boy was required to fend for himself and set out with a dog on a hunting expedition. After hunting all day without success, he decided to return home. On his return he came to a ridge where there were eight paths. Before he could decide which path to take, night fell and the boy died of hunger. He was, henceforth, known as *Susik Yongdong* and his spirit remained on earth to plague the human fetus, presumably causing it to die of hunger in the womb. The myth goes on to describe how the dog that accompanied the boy returned to *Tāpunāmā-Wāhināmā* with the news of her child's death. She began to cry and in her agony she went to look for her son. On discovering him, only his bones were left. She buried the bones and returned home. On her way she passed a large lake where she sat to rest. While resting, night came on and she fell asleep. In her dream her dead child's soul came and had intercourse with her. She was blinded by this act and soon died. Her spirit became the *Sugut* and remained on earth to cause women to die in childbirth.

Another myth is given to account for the origins of the *soghā* spirit. After the creation of the world, a boy and his sister decided to build a house. The boy went into the woods to cut a tree for the wood they needed. After repeated failures to cut the tree, his sister came to help him. She made offerings of food, liquor, and beer at the base of the tree and only then was the boy able to fell the tree. With the help of friends he brought it back to the village, and by accident it fell and killed his sister. For several nights the sister's spirit came to haunt her brother because he failed to give her a mourning feast. Finally, he called in a shaman who, with the help of his tutelary spirit, was able to trap the angry spirit. The spirit spoke to him and told him that she could only be held for three years at which point she would assume a number of forms that would be dangerous for the living. She would appear in the form of a bull's horns and kill unsuspecting men; she would enter trees and fall on people; she would sit in the mouth of a dog and bite people; or she would cause travelers to fall off trails and die. From that time forward, men have been plagued with accidental and violent deaths caused by *soghā* spirits. Only a shaman who knows the proper ritual is able to capture and control these spirits.

In the above mythological accounts unexpected and violent deaths are explained symbolically through the failures of men. Generally, such deaths originate with incestuous desire, greed, envy, or other asocial acts. These same qualities are attributed to the spirit forms—*soghā, sugut,* or *susik*. The Limbu identify evil in other contexts with similar asocial qualities of envy and jealousy. Suicide is thought to be the most extreme manifestation of these qualities. Indeed, death by "accident" or violence is equated with death by suicide; both result from the failures of men.

Death Rituals

The death rituals for those who die by suicide, violence, or childbirth parallel the mythological accounts. Such deaths are treated differently from normal deaths of old age or disease. In a normal death the deceased is washed, clothed, and laid out on a bamboo stretcher. An all-night vigil takes place over the body. On the following day, the body is carried to a cemetery. A grave is dug, and a coffin of rocks constructed in the base of the grave. The body is lowered into the grave, the coffin sealed, and the deceased's possessions are tossed on top of the coffin. The grave is filled and a marker placed on top. Following the funeral close relatives enter a period of mourning—four days for a male and three days for a female. During this period the immediate male relatives of the deceased, the sons, brothers, fathers, or husbands are isolated inside the deceased's home clothed only in a white cotton garment. They are not allowed to speak to non-patrilineal relatives or to eat foods coated in salt or oil. At the end of the mourning cycle a feast for the dead is prepared and attended by relatives, neighbors, and friends of the family. The principal mourners shave the hair from their bodies and sit in front of the feast while one or more shamans give a funeral oration to the guests. After the offerings have been made to the deceased's spirit, the guests are fed and the period of pollution is ended.

Without analyzing the details of this ritualized period of mourning, certain points emerge. All death is dangerous to the living, especially to close kinsmen. This danger is averted through prescribed ritual. Close relatives undergo a social death through isolation and are reborn at the mourning feast, where their connections to the deceased are severed. Death itself, though God-given and therefore unpredictable and inevitable, is made meaningful. Through ritual symbolism the living have exerted a control over death and reordered the universe by reaffirming social relations.

In abnormal deaths, the dangers are multiplied. Such deaths are brought about by human failure symbolized by the *soghā, sugut,* and *susik* spirits. In such situations, the entire world of man is threatened by disorder and inexplicable chaos. Society itself seems doomed by the forces of greed, envy, and jealousy. Because of these perceived dangers such deaths are given a different ritual treatment. I witnessed the procedures of such a death ritual only once while in the field. The following summarized account is presented as an illustration.

Death by Violence

After an extremely severe monsoon storm in the beginning of October, 1968, that lasted for three days and nights, my wife Shirley and I woke to learn that about midnight a landslide had crushed a house just below ours, killing two people, an old woman and a young girl of about three or four years. Three others in the house at the time had somehow escaped. When we arrived the bodies of the woman and young girl were laid out on bamboo stretchers on the front porch of the deceased woman's son's house, which was about 100 feet adjacent to the one that had been destroyed. A specialized shaman called a *mangba* had been called to the house along with his apprentice helper. The two were squatting under a tree facing the bodies. A number of onlookers (about 80 to 100 in all) had gathered at the scene. Unlike a normal Limbu funeral where those in attendance are almost invariably Limbus, most of whom are related by patrilineal descent or marriage, this crowd was multi-ethnic in composition. I noted several Brahmans and Chetris and a few Newar from the nearby Bazaar as well as representatives of the menial castes of leatherworkers, tailors and blacksmiths. The Limbus themselves were represented by many who were unrelated to the deceased either by marriage or descent. The crowd was a hodge-podge of curious people who happened to live close enough to witness the event. It was much like a crowd one would expect to find at a particularly disastrous car accident in Times Square, Manhattan—a congregation of the curious from all walks of life having little more in common than insatiable curiosity with death and a nearness to the disaster. I think this is worth mentioning because it demonstrates an important contrast between the two types of Limbu death rituals. At a normal funeral the attendance mirrors Limbu social structure in that the majority show a kinship relationship to the deceased. In an abnormal funeral the attendance reflects the unpredictable situation of chaos in the random and unordered composition of the crowd.

Shortly after we arrived, the shaman and his apprentice took charge of the proceedings. They began to chant and beat their percussion instruments, a drum and brass plate. Almost as a signal the bodies were lifted and carried along a path towards the ridge above followed by the crowd. The shamans danced on the spot where the bodies had lain and followed the funeral procession, beating their instruments constantly. At the top of the ridge near a Limbu cemetery, the procession stopped. The *mangba* ran to several of the graves, danced around them, and returned to the crowd. The procession then continued past the cemetery along a path leading into a forested area. The shaman and his apprentice followed, repetitiously chanting and drumming. In a clearing in the forested area the entire procession stopped and several men began immediately, without ceremony, to dig the graves. While the digging was in process, the crowd sat near the bodies talking and chatting amidst the wailing of close relatives. On completion of the work, the bodies were rapidly lowered into the grave. Their eyes, ears, and noses were covered. I was told later that they were buried face down.

Again the contrasts to a normal funeral should be noted. In a normal funeral the bodies are laid near the grave while it is being dug and their faces shaded by a white cloth; in the abnormal funeral, the bodies are unshaded. In a normal funeral, a coffin of stones is constructed in the grave; in the one witnessed above, no coffin was constructed. In a normal burial, the bodies are buried face up in an extended position; in the one under description, they are buried face down. In a normal burial the orifices of the body are uncovered; in an abnormal funeral, the eyes, ears, and nose are covered. Finally, in a normal funeral, the deceased is buried in a cemetery in a plot "purchased" and consecrated by a shaman; in an abnormal funeral, the deceased is buried in a grave dug in the forest and the plot is neither "purchased" nor consecrated by the shaman. In a normal funeral the grave is marked; in the one being described, the grave is left unmarked.

After the burial, the procession broke into confusion. The participants engaged in a mock battle with sticks on the path leading back towards the ridge past the cemetery. This particular mock battle threatened to lead to a real fight when two of the participants began to hit each other in earnest, each claiming that the other had hit him in anger rather than in jest. They were controlled by the crowd, which had by this time reached a crossroads leading back to the scene of the accident. The shaman and his apprentice again took control of the procession. The *mangba* sacrificed a chicken and placed it next to a bottle of liquor in the middle of the road, as an offering to the spirits of the dead woman and child.

The *mangba* and his apprentice began to dance around the offering, simulating a trance, with the stated purpose of sealing off the road to prevent the *soghā* spirits from escaping. No one was allowed to stand between the offering and the burial ground, for fear the spirits, who were not yet fully under the control of the *mangba*, might attach themselves to the unfortunate participant. On completion of this rite, the *mangba* then marked each participant on the forehead with a piece of charcoal as a protection against the powers of the *soghā* spirit. Many who had accompanied the procession returned to their homes. The remainder followed the *mangba* in procession back to the house of the deceased woman's son.

On arrival at the house, the shaman and his apprentice danced around the house. Again chaos broke out. Many of the onlookers standing in a terraced field just above the courtyard of the house began throwing pumpkins, squashes, and other garden produce on those unfortunate enough to be standing in the courtyard. The deceased woman's son tossed many of the dead woman's possessions into the pile of debris. In the middle of this confusion two men dragged a squealing pig that belonged to the deceased into the courtyard and decapitated it with a Nepali bushknife, basking many of the onlookers with the blood of the animal. The *mangba* and his apprentice continued their dance on the front porch of the house. A number of women strained beer for those in the procession as is customary after a normal burial. Many drank their beer and went home. A few stayed to assist in the preparations for the ritual to capture and "kill" the *soghā* spirits, which was to take place during the night. Gradually, the crowd diminished and the few that remained sat around discussing the events that had taken place. The lull continued until nightfall. After a short spell, I went to my house and ate.

When I returned shortly after dark, the meat from the slaughtered pig was being prepared for the fifteen or twenty people who remained. All were Limbus, but only about half were related to the deceased. The *mangba* and his apprentice sat on the porch of the house, smoking and drinking beer, waiting for the meal to be prepared. Others were cutting and stripping bamboo to be used in the construction of a special altar in the courtyard of the deceased's woman's son's house.

A bonfire was lit, and a few feet from it, a small mound about four to six feet in diameter and about 3 or 4 inches in height was erected. On this mound two large bamboo branches about 10 to 12 feet high were crossed and tied together. From the ground to the point where the branches crossed, a 3-step ladder was built. Circling the edge of the mound, a small "x"-shaped fence was constructed and left open at one end. A cloth banner and sword were stuck into the mound near the base of the branches, and oil flames, a leaf-plate of rice, and a vase of flowers completed the altar. A small hole about 6 inches in depth was scooped out next to the altar. The *soghā* spirits were to be lured into this hole and "killed" by fire.

After the *mangba* had eaten he entered the house and began chanting. While he chanted, the sons of the deceased woman strung two small necklaces (*mālā*) of seed pods and placed them on the altar as symbols of those who had just been killed. The *mangba* then approached the altar in the courtyard and seated himself in front of the opening. The apprentice sat next to him and began drumming. Gradually, the drumming and chanting increased until both men arose and began a dance around the altar. At the climax of the dance, the *mangba* blew a bone whistle intended to summon the *soghā* spirits. The dance continued for fifteen or twenty minutes until the two shamans sat down to rest in front of the altar. They repeated this procedure on occasion until long past midnight, with the stated purpose of gradually gaining control over the *soghā* spirits.

Finally, at about 3:00 a.m., one of the women brought a dish of corn flour that was heated over the fire, while another participant lit three bamboo torches. The *mangba* and his helper arose and began to beat the brass plate. An onlooker grabbed the banner and sword from the altar and flailed them wildly about. Another grabbed a long stick and beat it randomly in the air. Suddenly, the shaman and helper ran around the house followed by the holders of the torches, the corn flour, and the weapons. The procession continued past the house that had been destroyed and up the trail towards the top of the ridge, flinging the corn flour at the torches and beating at the *soghā* spirits. A fence of fire was erected at the crossroads, and the *soghā* spirits were chased by the group towards the altar. When the group, led by the shamans, returned to the altar, coals from the fire were casually tossed into the hole where the *soghā* spirits were thought to have hidden, and the performance ended. The participants drank beer and went home.

The funeral for those killed by the landslide ended with the above events. No period of mourning was observed, nor did the surviving relatives observe a period of fasting or the costumary pollution rites. A mourning feast for the dead was ignored.

The expressed purpose of the entire ritual described above was to "kill" the *soghā* spirits. During my questioning of the events, I learned that the phrase, "to kill the spirits," was only a metaphor for "capturing" them, since a spirit cannot be killed in a literal sense. Depending upon the powers of the *mangba* and upon his having performed the ritual properly, the spirits remain harmless for three years. At the end of each three-year period the ritual must be repeated to insure the safety of those living in the vicinity of the accident. If the *mangba* fails in his performance, the spirits remain loose and harass the living, possibly causing further deaths by violence.

CONCLUSIONS

The death ritual just described emphasizes in dramatic fashion the chaos unleashed by unexpected death in Limbu society. This chaos is symbolized again and again in events that lead up to the "killing" of the *soghā* spirits. The entire ritual oscillates between periods of social and psychological chaos and systematic exertion of control over the participant's behavior by the shaman and his apprentice. The ritual is punctuated and held together by the shaman's chanting, drumming, and dancing. The role of the shaman is to bring order to a society threatened by unexpected and unpredictable death. In this capacity he functions as both political and religious leader. He controls the participants by leading them from one stage of the ritual to the next, and in his final act of "killing" the *soghā* spirits, he exerts control over the supernatural realm.

The ritual itself, from beginning to end, may be likened to a dramatic performance designed to stamp out death or, at the very least, to make death intelligible, meaningful, and predictable. It might be described quite simply as a symbolic battle with death. Death, especially death by accident or violence, is the mask of a chaotic universe, a "universe in ruins." The death ritual is the Limbu's attempt to capture and order this chaos in his own terms.

In the death ritual "chaos vs. order" is symbolized in a number of instances. The bodies are buried in the forest rather than a cemetery, showing the contrast between unordered and ordered space. The funeral occurs immediately without delay and without a period of mourning or pollution, thereby contrasting time in terms of the unexpected and the expected. A mock battle ensues, emphasizing anarchy as opposed to an ordered society.

Underneath the symbolism of this death ritual is a reality that cannot be tolerated for any length of time by the human mind—the reality that life has no other purpose than "being." The symbolism does not express this reality; it denies it. By contrasting chaos and order, the ritual offers a dialectical synthesis of the two and tells us finally that the situation of death itself is now under control. God and man are once again in charge. An imperfect world of chaos, inexplicable events, and anarchy are replaced by order, explanations, and social control.

CHAPTER 4

Freud, Durkheim, and Death Among the Sebei[1]

Walter Goldschmidt

The ritual aspects of Sebei funerary customs are not simply more concerned with the living than with the dead; they are directed almost entirely to the living, giving but cursory attention to the body and none whatsoever to the soul of the deceased. It is my purpose here to show why this direction of ritual attention to the survivors should be the case.

As the title suggests, I have a further agenda. I believe that the function of ritual is to serve as a mediating force between the private motivations of individual actors and the structural relationships created by the social context in which these take place. Thus, Freud in my title represents symbolically the inner motivations of individual actors and the emotions these invoke, while Durkheim expresses those structural situations which create role demands and expectations. We will return to this at the close.

SEBEI FUNERAL PRACTICES

I must first very briefly describe Sebei funerary practices. In olden times, the Sebei placed the dead in a bushy place for the hyenas to devour. This was ideally done by the next brother; the body was positioned according to custom. Now, the body is interred near the house where refuse is thrown; it is washed, wrapped in sheeting, and some of the more personal possessions placed in the grave. This is all done very quickly. When the body is placed in the grave, it is made comfortable as a body, but nothing is made available for the soul; there is no libation of beer or bit of meat or words of encouragement. The items placed in the grave are those most intimately associated with the living body; his clothes and bedding. They are not the things he might wish to possess in some postmortem existence—not even the beer straw he had always carried with him. It is to be done the day of his death or before the cattle are released the next morning. After the funeral, those involved with handling the body are cleansed.

[1] This paper was read at the Annual Meeting of the American Anthropological Association in New York in November, 1971. The present paper is based on research done in 1961-1962 under grant G11713 from the National Science Foundation, and grant MH04097 from the National Institute of Mental Health, and on earlier work supported by The Wenner-Gren Foundation and the SSRC.

The major ceremony takes place on the fourth day; it is called chasing away the death. The ritual aspects are devoted to matters that can only be viewed as purification of the mourners. Involved are the slaughter of a bull from the herd of the deceased and the distribution of the meat, shaving the heads of the mourners, including the widows, the brothers and adult sons and their wives, strewing the chyme on the path by which the mourners go to the stream to bathe, the bathing, and the anointing of the personal possessions of the deceased before these are given to those who will take them. When these rituals are completed, there is a public hearing on the debts of the deceased, of which more will be said below.

The widows and the brother who will inherit them remain in seclusion and under restrictions on certain food, and certain forms of behavior, including sexual intercourse. The nature of these restrictions suggests that they are dangerous to themselves and to others during this liminal period. These restrictions are removed by a ceremony, involving the slaughter of a ram, the cooking of a stew involving parts of this animal and the interdicted food, and sexual intercourse by the heir with each of the wives in the order of their marriage. This last is called "cleaning out the ashes," in reference to the ashes which are said to have been sprinkled on her head and in her vagina at the earlier ceremony. If it was not done at the ritual of chasing away the death, then there will be a final determination as to which brother or brothers will inherit the widows. There may be a later ceremony to unify the herd of the deceased with that of the inheriting son.

The ceremonial is replete with symbols of cleansing; universal ones such as washing, running streams, fire and ashes, the right and left paths, and the removal of that most obvious human growth, hair; culture-specific ones, such as the chyme and fat of slaughtered animals, the use of certain medicinal roots and vines. Even the ritual of sexual intercourse (which might have been viewed as defiling) is expressed in the idiom of cleansing. I would also see that ancient symbol of Orpheus and Job, the tabu against looking back, as being in this context a fear of the evil inherent in death, not the spirit of the deceased, that is the focus of concern.

What is striking about this set of rituals is not the involvement with purification, which is, after all, widespread if not universal, but the failure to show concern about the soul. The soul is not mentioned; nothing is made available for it; it is not protected against, prevented from returning, spurred on to distant worlds, placated, or enticed. The ceremony is called chasing away *death*—not the soul—and there is every reason to believe that psychologically and metaphysically it is death that is feared, not the spirit of the deceased. Later, when the deceased has become a clan ancestor, he will be placated with libations and sweet words, but nothing of this sort is done at the funeral. The closely related Nandi say that the soul's way to the afterlife is through the hyena's intestines, but the Sebei say no such thing. (Hollis, 1907, p. 7.) The Sebei, incidentally, have an inordinate fear of death, and much of their ritual life is directed to a protection against the dangers inherent in the physical or spiritual environment. (Edgerton, 1971, p. 119.)

Our task is therefore to understand, first, why there is such a strong sense of defilement, and second, why this has so little reference to the deceased.

THE FUNERAL MOOT

In order to understand this, we must go back to the legal matters that are raised in the moots associated with funerals. The Sebei engage in very complex exchanges of cattle and other property, which I shall not try to describe here. (Goldschmidt, 1967, Chapter 11.) These exchanges have important economic functions in herd management, which the Sebei themselves fully recognize. Any man of substance is a party to a number of such exchanges, so that at the time of his death, there will be indebtednesses that are encumberances on the estate and payments due to it. The creditors must make a public claim against the estate at the time of the funeral rite; a person failing to do so forfeits his claim. Thus, every funeral is not merely a ritual, but also a court of law. For a very rich man, the claims involved may take hours to resolve, and in those instances I watched, there were some disputes that were not resolved. (Goldsschmidt, 1969, passim.)

There is also the matter of inheritance of property. The personal possessions (stool, spears, etc.) do not create any problems once they have been ritually purified. But the livestock and land are another matter. A man's herd is a complicated set of rights and obligations, not merely so many cattle, sheep, and goats. Subsidiary rights to some have been allocated to each of his wives, and these can only go to her sons, while some are not so allocated. In addition to legal claims, there are also moral ones. All this means that the inheritance is by no means automatic, and decisions must be reached. Only in the case of a very poor man would there be no such decisions to make; for a man of importance these may take days to resolve, as is amply demonstrated in *Kambuya's Cattle*, which is the verbatim record of one such moot (Goldschmidt, 1969). These matters, too, should be settled at the hearings in association with the funeral.

Finally there are the wives who are to be inherited. This involves two sets of considerations. While there are theoretical regulations as to who will take the widows, the actual outcome can become very complicated through ancillary rules. We may be certain that this invokes deep-felt sentiments on the part of the potential heirs, on the part of the widows, and, as I discovered at one funeral, on the part of her adolescent sons. We may be reasonably sure that this welter of sentiments will be far from univocal, that there will be division of opinion, concern, disappointment, anger, jealousy: the man who is supposed to inherit may not want the burdens; a widow may desire a brother who finds a reason not to become the heir, and a son may feel ashamed (I was told) that "his mother has so many husbands." To this emotion-laden problem some solution must be found during the period of mourning. These difficulties are further exacerbated in that part of Sebei where cultivation is important, for the inheritance of widows also involves de facto control of the farm lands. While legally the heir merely holds such land in trust for the minor sons of the deceased, he does in fact have the benefit of its use during the interval. Today, if the land is planted in coffee, he gets the cash income during that period.

We see, therefore, that the Sebei have utilized the heightened emotional tensions that are evoked by the presence of death to settle a variety of extremely important and complicated legal matters. Those who come to the funeral—and they *must* be present—do not come merely as mourners, but as litigants, prepared to further their personal interests as these have been affected by the death.

Viewed from the standpoint of Sebei contractual law, the public hearings that take place in conjunction with the funerary rites will be seen as a functionally effective device for preserving the record in a nonliterate community and assuring the equitable satisfaction of economic obligations and rights. The existence of the contractual arrangements, with respect to cattle, is, in turn, a functionally effective device for spreading risks, sharing resources, and establishing collaborative action in legal, as well as economic, matters. (Goldschmidt, 1967, pp. 191-192) Viewed, however, from the perspective provided by the occasion of a death, it can be seen that this custom places a particular emotional burden on the mourners, provoking their cupidity and rousing them to engage in behavior which is laden with potential conflict and hostility, at the very moment when their sentiments should be otherwise.

DISCUSSION

The anthropological discourse on death rituals has generally centered around the notion that they are performed to regain equilibrium that has been disrupted by the death. That they perform this function is not to be denied. But this viewpoint is generally stated in a kind of passive mood, indirectly articulating the notion of a reified society rearranging its sociological feathers. Thus, for instance, Radcliffe-Brown (1933, p. 285) writes: "Mourning customs [are] the means by which the social sentiments of the survivors are slowly reorganized and adapted to the new conditions produced by the death." This view disregards the important fact that this rearrangement is not accomplished by a passive "society," but by a very active set of actors, who enter the arena set by the funeral with the clear intent of seeking resolution of conflicts that are structured into the situation.

But to recognize this fact is to take cognizance of individual motivation and the emotional burden that these invoke. The fact that the individuals are, in the presence of death, actually concerned with their own welfare—must be so concerned—evokes in them a strong sense of guilt. Freud, in *Thoughts on War and Death*, (1956, p. 305) has written: "Least of all will [a person] permit himself to think of the death of another if with that event some gain to himself in freedom, means or position is connected."

Paul Ricoeur, in *The Symbolism of Evil*, has suggested that the sense of defilement derives from the feelings of vengeance and that this bond between evil and misfortune involves the anticipation of punishment. (Ricoeur, 1967, p. 7) I believe that the nexus he proposes is vitally important, and that the emotions inherent in a situation are projected onto the larger screen of culture in forms that we call religious symbolism. This is, I think, the basis for understanding the focus on ritual purification of the mourners.

Why, however, does this involve so little concern with the deceased? It is because the antagonisms, hostilities, and confrontations that take place at a funeral are directed at other survivors and not at the dead man. They have been released by the *fact* of the death, but they involve the conflicts of interest among the fellow survivors. Thus it is that the dead man relinquishes center stage, while death itself is the source of the evil sentiments that suffuse the mourning scene. The cupidity it invokes and the guilt that results are defiling to the actors who remove it by rites of purification.

An exceptional bit of behavior of one mourner throws this relationship into relief. At the moot, his claim against the estate of his brother (the loan of 100 E. A. shillings with coffee land as security) was brought forward. He announced that he was going to forfeit this claim, an act of generosity unique in my experience. This man earlier had made disparaging remarks at the expressions of grief and other ritual actions, but when his brother was being lowered into the grave, he could not bear to watch, and absented himself until the grave had been filled. Not being able to accept these ritual acts made it impossible for him to cope with his own sentiments which he then ameliorated by not taking anything from his brother's estate.

We may sum up this discussion by saying that the Sebei structure the situation in such a way that the individual mourners are forced to play dirty, and that it follows that they want to cleanse themselves.

BROADER IMPLICATIONS

I now want to return to Freud and Durkheim and the role of ritual in social life. I think it is clear that the structural analysis of the situation plays an important role in the matter of funeral practices, but that it cannot provide us with an adequate explanation of their form and character without a consideration of human motivations and sentiments. Contrariwise, those who would seek to understand ritual acts in terms simply of human psychological characteristics find that they cannot do so. Thus the psychoanalyst John Bowlby (1961, pp. 328-331) bolsters his notions of grief with—of all things—anecdotes about animal behavior.

The Sebei behavior does not only suggest that the understanding of ritual requires an appreciation of both facets. To me, at least, it suggests that there is a tension created between the private and personal interests of the individual and the situational demands created by the structure of the society. Such tensions would place an intolerable burden upon the individual in the absence of a mechanism for their release. Rituals act as a means of defusing this tension, disarming the potential disruption created by such structural conflict. If a ritual is to perform this function, it must relate realistically to the private, though culturally induced, desires of the individual and the structural requirements of the social order. This, I believe, is what the Sebei funeral rites are designed to accomplish; this, I believe, is a general function of ritual.

REFERENCES

Bowlby, John. Processes of mourning. *The International Journal of Psycho-Analysis*, 1961, 42:317-340.

Edgerton, Robert. *The individual in cultural adaptation: a study of four east african peoples*. Berkeley and Los Angeles: University of California Press, 1971.

Freud, Sigmund. *Thoughts for the times on war and death*. Trans. by Joan Riviere. In *Collected papers 4*. The Hogarth Press and the Institute of Psycho-Analysis, 1956.

Goldschmidt, Water. *Sebei law*. Berkeley and Los Angeles: University of California Press, 1967.

———. Kambuya's cattle: the legacy of an African herdsman. Berkeley and Los Angeles: University of California Press, 1969.

Hollis, A. C. *The Nandi, their language and fold-lore*. Oxford: Clarendon Press, 1909.

Radcliffe-Brown, A. R. *The Andaman Islanders*, 2nd ed. Cambridge: The University Press, 1933.

Ricouer, Paul. *The symbolism of evil*. New York, Evanston and London: Harper & Row, 1969.

CHAPTER
5

The Good Death in Kaliai: Preparation for Death in Western New Britain*

David R. Counts

The institutionalization of death and the dehumanization of the dying has become something of a *cause célèbre* in North American society. The jobs of caring for the aged and infirm traditionally assigned to families have in our society now passed largely into the hands of bureaucratized bodies; with that care also has passed the responsibility for preparation for death. And therein is a problem. It seems not so much that preparation for death is done badly as that it is hardly done at all.

Melanesian Death-Related Behavior

Without proposing a prescription and with no suggestion that the data presented here can serve as a model against which to measure our own performance, I wish in this chapter to examine preparation for death and the folk theories that sustain death-related behaviour among an isolated Melanesian people.

The Kaliai are a Melanesian-speaking people numbering about one thousand.

* Material in this paper was gathered during two periods of field research in West New Britain. The research was generously supported by the U.S. National Science Foundation and Southern Illinois University (1966-67), and by a grant from the Canada Council (S71-1701) and McMaster University (1971).

They comprise one of five linguistic groups occupying the Kaliai census sub-division on the north coast of the West New Britain District in Papua New Guinea. They dwell nowadays in five coastal villages fronting on the Bismarck Sea. The Kaliai were first contacted by whites around the turn of the century, but the succeeding decades have seen them remain on the fringes of even such little development as was occurring in New Guinea. The thrust of mission colonialism reached them shortly after contact, but with the interruption of the two wars, no resident priest dwelt among them until 1949. Almost all of the Kaliai are now converted to Roman Catholicism, but the conversions are more of form than substance. Little of traditional ritual and religious practice seems to have gone out of use, and none has been forgotten.

KALIAI THEORIES OF DEATH

In this chapter, I wish to develop a number of points which characterize the beliefs held by Kaliai concerning death and dying, beliefs which require the living, the dying, and the dead to behave toward each other in particular ways.

Death is not an end to life, but a transition between different life states— Those who experience bodily death are passing through one stage in the transformation from human (*iavava*) to non-human (*antu*) life. Once the transformation is complete, *antu* have little active interest in the lives of *iavava,* but the separation between the two kinds of beings is never complete. Human beings who have not experienced death have contact with *antu* only at their peril. *Antu* are normally invisible to human beings and are infinitely more powerful than they, being capable of flight, of taking animal form, of tele-porting material objects, and being in control of great wealth. But in no sense are they spirits. *Antu* have corporeal form, they carry out the daily round of gardening for food, fishing, carrying water; they must build houses, they marry, and occasionally they beget children. *Antu* are, in short, superhuman beings. On occasion, they dispense with their cloak of invisibility and engage in intercourse with ordinary persons. Kaliai myths recount the consequences of such instances. In one myth, an *antu* woman lured by the aphrodisiac ointment of an ordinary man became visible to him, and their subsequent marriage and attempt to live a normal life in a human village led to a disastrous war between *iavava* and *antu* and the firm re-establishment of the boundary of invisibility [1].

*The transition from human life through bodily death to super human life is not instantaneous. Death requires time for the severing of social relationships in the normal world. The separation process may either precede or follow the event of bodily death. There is extreme danger in those rare cases where the transition cannot be completed—*Bodily death is a natural event which all persons must experience, but for the Kaliai death becomes a social event signalling the time-consuming transformation process only for those persons who have become fully social beings. Thus the death of very young children who have not been integrated in the web of the society is an essentially private event. The Kaliai mark the boundary between infancy and full humanity (requiring death ritual) with regard to a child's ability to discuss his dream life. The death of a child who has not yet acquired both language and the perception of a difference between waking and dreaming events may bring grief to his parents, but it is not a matter of social concern. These principles also explain the apparent lack of negative sanctions regarding infanticide. Death through exposure was prescribed for unnatural births, a category which included not only deformed infants, but multiple births, and no mortuary rites followed such action.

For fully human beings, however, the event of bodily death requires the severing of the social relationships which have bound the dying persons to others in the society. In classic Melanesian fashion, the social relationships which bind persons together in Kaliai are most commonly expressed through an imbalanced flow of the material goods which constitute wealth. In the simplest, economic sense everyone in Kaliai society is debtor to some, creditor to others. The manipulation of one's ties of kin and affinity to occasion the flow of large amounts of wealth is the primary route to prestige and political leadership in Kaliai society. Hence the greater the political status of the person facing or experiencing bodily death, the more entangled and extensive are his exchange relations likely to be. When death is apprehended or experienced it is necessary that the imbalance be corrected—that the lines of flow be reversed and brought to a steady state, severing the social as well as the economic ties. Until such severance has been completed, a dead person retains his interest in the affairs of ordinary mortals and his transformation into new *antu* life status remains incomplete.

If the coming of bodily death is seen beforehand, every effort is made to accomplish the severance process in advance of the event of death. But a person who has lived an active social life has entangled himself in many social relationships and the process of separation is likely to be lengthy. Thus Kaliai political leaders (*Maroni*) are likely to slacken their exchange activities and enter semi-retirement from active leadership as they reach advanced age. However, the attractions of power and honour to one's name are great enough that only rarely does a person succeed in conducting his own severance of social relationships.

Much more commonly death occurs before the completion of the separation, and the task is left to the heirs of the deceased. Such is a primary function of the extensive round of mortuary exchanges that constitute the cycle known as *ololo* among the Kaliai. In a lengthy series of ritual stages the heritable property of the deceased person is distributed among his heirs and all of his obligations are terminated. Only on its completion is the spirit free of its human individuality and thus of its tendency to be drawn as a ghost back into human affairs.

Not infrequently, of course, death comes to a person with little or no warning. The Kaliai face many dangers to life and these can strike quickly. The sea on their doorstep abounds with threats to life—shark, barracuda, lethally poisonous fish and shell fish, crocodiles—while debilitating diseases remain endemic: malaria, yaws, tuberculosis, dengue, to name only a few. What should be underscored here is that Kaliai believe death resulting from the potential causes noted above, as well as from a host of other sources including accident, is the consequence of the active violation of a person's right to longevity and a good death following upon the severance of social relationships. Whatever the immediate cause of death, the ultimate cause of every death which comes in advance of the readiness of the dying person is the malevolence of some sentient being. Death almost never merely comes— rather, almost always, it is sent. Hence, for the Kaliai it is possible to describe a good death and a bad death.

A good death in Kaliai is one which comes with the acquiescence of the dying person and after sufficient time for the severance of social relationships— While it is possible to formulate the foregoing statement with some confidence, the statement should not be taken to imply either that Kaliai seek death or that the good death comes with ease or frequency. In the preceding section I noted that Kaliai attribute most deaths to an active agent as cause. The number of possible agents is quite restricted: other humans may kill either through direct action or may kill through the practice of *muso* (sorcery); autochthonous beings who inhabit the surrounding region may inflict death for infringement of their rights or, sometimes, merely through caprice; and ghosts of the dead, either those not fully transformed into *antu* or, more rarely, *antu* themselves, may cause death to human beings who offend them. For a Kaliai to live so circumspectly that he does not run afoul of someone or something (and thus attract death) verges on the impossible. Yet a story is told of one who escaped killing to die the good death. When the man had lived to a great age without having given mortal offense to any being, he began to feel as though his body was wearing out. He called all his kinsmen to gather around him, disposed of his possessions after repaying the obligations owed by him and forgiving any obligations of others to him, and then informed those gathered that it was time for him to die. When they began to grieve, he told them that they should not, for his life was complete and he was experiencing no pain. Then he described the coming of death as, one by one, his bones crumbled and, at last, a shapeless mass of flesh, the body died. His relatives buried him and there were no mortuary rites.

What militates against the achievement of a good death for nearly everyone is that the behaviour required of every person passing through a normal life

cycle in Kaliai society assures that at some point he or she will offend someone or something, either by a violation of rights, the causing of shame, or
the arousal of envy sufficient to cause the other to kill the offender. Nearly
everyone, then, dies before his time, being torn out of his web of relationships
and leaving it to his survivors to finish the task of balancing the flow.

*A Kaliai perceiving his death approaching, exerts whatever control he can
over the severance of his social ties*—The perception of death by a Kaliai is not
the same as acquiescence in its coming. Perception of death entails recognition
that unless the course of events perceived to be entrained is altered, one must
be prepared to die. The signalling of this knowledge is by public action
initiated by the supposedly dying person: his removal from the enclosed space
in which he is housed to an open temporary shelter or tent (NM: *haus sel*).
The activity that follows such a removal is directed to two complementary
ends:

1. An attempt to ascertain and thwart the cause of death.
2. Efforts to initiate the bringing of closure to the dying person's social
   relationships in event of the failure to thwart death.

The attempt to ascertain and thwart the cause of death is continuous as
the victim sees his death approaching. Every avenue is explored—the white
man's medicines as well as the operations of curers in the villages—but the
theory of the cause of illness and death leads to expectations that are seldom
met by the curative efforts. Inasmuch as illness and death are attributed to
the actions of a sentient agent, only a dramatic remission of symptoms is
immediately recognized as success. As a result, in most cases, the attempt at
medical treatment is paced by continued preparation for death.

Preparation for death as outlined here has as an important element the
gathering of all those with whom the social relations of the victim are in
imbalance. Such gatherings are often quite large and so are usually
incompatible with hospital treatment of the victim's complaint. In consequence,
a person expecting death goes to hospital reluctantly, and if no immediately
apparent success is attained by medical treatment, he will leave at the first
opportunity. Leaving hospital without being cured is almost invariably a
signal for the pitching of a sail shelter and the onset of grieving by relatives.
The victim is centered under the sail, surrounded by the crowd and ministered
to by close relatives or various curers. The conversation, however, is *about* the
victim, not with him. People speculate on the identity of the killer, examine
the victim's behaviour for transgressions and argue over the facts of his
financial life. Women engage in economic exchange on a much smaller scale
than men, and, when the dying person is a woman, the speculation is much
more likely to focus on her husband's affairs and offences than it is on her
own. The dying person participates to the extent allowed by his illness,

especially with regard to the settlement of argument over matters of fact pertaining to his financial affairs.

As might be suspected, the above course of events often ends, not in death, but in the gradual recovery of the victim. No shame is attached to mistaken apprehension of death, and the person simply resumes his life as before. If death does ensue the same persons who have been ministering to the dying person continue their ministrations to the remains—bathing, dressing and cradling the dead person in their arms—while at the same time giving full voice to their grief in a crying chant. These activities continue through (today) the preparation of a coffin and the preparation of a grave site.

My concern here has been with the apprehension of death and the way in which Kaliai prepare for its arrival, not with their behavior after death's arrival takes place. I have tried to show that their behavior arises from a set of ordered principles which define the nature of dying, the causes of death and the relation between the living and the dead. The goal of the behavior is to escape the problems resulting from a bad death. It should be noted that the avoidance of these problems is to the advantage of both the dying person and to his survivors. For the dying person, translation into the spirit world is speeded. For the living survivors, the difficulties of dealing with a restless ghost are avoided.

REFERENCE

1. D. E. A. Counts, Akro and Gagandewa, *The Journal of Symbolic Anthropology*, Mouton, The Hague, in press.

PART 2
Death
in
The United States
and
Mexico

The process of dying, the meaning of death, the beliefs in what happens after death: each of these varies as a function of a variety of factors, one of which is the particular subculture or subcultures with which the individual identifies and affiliates. The United States and Canada are relatively new nations, most of whose citizens have grandparents born in other countries. The history of these nations is also the history of people leaving other lands and settling here; some of these settlers lost much of their identification with their homelands, but many others did not. Ethnic identification is strong, therefore, among the descendents of the Finns in Minnesota, the Japanese in California, the Puerto Ricans in New York, the Italians in Massachusetts, the French in Quebec, the Swedes in Washington, the Mexicans in Texas, the Irish in Ontario, and the Blacks throughout North America. At the same time, pockets of early settlers became isolated and developed their own equivalent of ethnic identification: the Northern Europeans in Appalachia, the Hispanics in New Mexico, the East European Jews in numerous urban centers, the Native Americans on isolated reservations.

All of this has added up to an immense variety of cultural influences on views, values, and behavior involving death, dying, and bereavement. It is so little talked about, however, that many individuals are unaware of the diversity. And, of course, further diversity is added as the result of religion, of region, and of cultural assimilation, so that it is often difficult to know whether the beliefs of a particular individual are more closely related to ethnicity, religion, region, or idiosyncratic preferences.

Very little research has probed into ethnic differences, although a handful of studies have been reported (1, 2) and others will undoubtedly be forthcoming. What is most important is the recognition that cultural identification matters very much. Thus each ethnic community in North America has had a different history with death in their present homeland, as well as a different history in their community or origin. The following articles provide a historical overview of three ethnic communities: Blacks in the United States, Mexicans and persons of Mexican ancestry, and both rural and urban residents of Kentucky. In each instance, some of the contemporary subcultural views reflect their ancestry, some reflect their North American history, and some reflect their present circumstances.

Culture influences death concerns in virtually every way possible: it affects causes of death and the kinds of care that dying people receive; it influences perceptions of health caretakers and the methods used by health caretakers and who is entitled to be a health caretaker; it determines funeral rituals and burial rituals and whether remains are disposed of by earth, water, or fire; it has an effect on where the dying occurs, who is in attendance, and how the body is handled after death. It is impossible to exaggerate the role of culture.

And there are often subcultures within subcultures. Many people will talk about the Black American view of death or the Hispanic funeral rituals, but the Blacks in the rural south may view death much differently than the Blacks in the urban Northeast, while the Hispanics whose roots in New Mexico extend for 300 years have different traditions than those who have come to southern California within the past ten years.

Age is another important factor, since older people within a subculture often have more vivid memories of their cultural heritage, while younger people are more influenced by what they see around them, even though many younger people express eagerness to return to their ethnic traditions.

Finally, of course, are individual differences within any group. Within every ethnic community will be people who fear death and people who do not, people who adhere to traditional funerary rituals and people who despise the traditional, people who wish to utilize modern medical sciences and facilities and medicines as much as possible and people who are suspicious of the efficacy of all these. Thus, understanding cultures and subcultures can go a long way to help in understanding those who identify with them, but it is also important not to lose sight of the substantial differences among individuals within any subculture.

1. Bengtson, V. L., Cuellar, J. B., & Ragan, P. K. Stratum contrasts and similarities in attitudes toward death. *Journal of Gerontology,* 1977, *32,* 76-88.
2. Kalish, R. A., & Reynolds, D. K. *Death and ethnicity: A psychocultural study.* Los Angeles: University of Southern California Press, 1976.

Death Shall Have
No Dominion:
The Passing of
the World of
the Dead in America

Charles O. Jackson

In this century, at least for Americans, connection between the world of the dead and that of the living has been largely severed and the dead world is disappearing. Communion between the two realms has come to an end. It is a radical departure because for three centuries prior, life and death were not held apart. Meaning flowed freely between the two worlds. It is radical also in that the movement toward withdrawal from the dead reversed a strong trend apparent through most of the nineteenth century, in which the place and role of the dead in the world of the living was increasing significantly.

Death in Victorian America

That trend itself was a consequence of the decline in what has been called the "Pilgrim posture" toward life [1, 2]. In this view the world was merely a wilderness to be suffered as preparation for the truly significant "eternal" home. But that posture gradually weakened. Even though the Pilgrim rhetoric continued, death was increasingly perceived in the first half of the nineteenth century within a context of growing attachment to the "wilderness" as well as some unease about the true future of the dead. As death became less and less acceptable, the living demanded that it be domesticated, its harsh reality muted and beautified. The living became more unwilling to conclude their relationship with those departed. They would also seek comfort through a substantial reduction in social distance between the dead world and the living world. Indeed, at least by the last quarter of the nineteenth century the two realms had become highly intertwined.

One dramatic expression of this movement was to be found in the antebellum graveyard. In the eighteenth century there were few who concerned themselves with the location of human remains. The dead could not, and the living committed to the "Pilgrim posture" did not either. From that perspective the body was unimportant, no more than a shell to be readily abandoned at the conclusion of one's earthly travail. By the third decade of the nineteenth century, however, the dead were becoming precious. The result for the graveyard was the "rural cemetery movement." While the initial motivation for this application of landscape gardening techniques to the graveyard was considerations of public health, much more than sanitation was expected of the new burial grounds. The dead would be rescued from crowded, appalling conditions of many earlier yards and would now receive appropriate respect. Amid this beautiful and rustic environment with personalized plots there would be positive proof for both the dead and the living that the latter truly cared. The cemeteries would also become popular recreational parks for the living who found in them a source of assurance, succor, and moral instruction.

Nor was the cemetery the only evidence and example of the closing between the dead and living worlds in the nineteenth century. Personal care of the body of the deceased had always been a prime responsibility of family and friends. This continued through the century. The home was the typical location of the wake and became so for the funeral. Professional undertaking services obtained growing popularity by the latter years of that century, but the responsibility over the body which the family was willing to delegate to such a functionary was limited. Many clearly felt that the body deserved more respect than to be handed over to strangers for final disposition. What became significantly new in the relationship with the dead was the increased attention and resources which the living world gave to preservation and aesthetic presentation of the body. Even by the early nineteenth century there was growing public interest in receptacles which would provide greater and more durable protection for the corpse than did the currently standard simple wood coffin. Certainly by the eve of the Civil War there was a clear and increasing demand for containers whose claim to acceptability lay flatly in the fact that they were beautiful, inside and outside [3, Chapter 7]. The significance of such trends in body receptacles was epitomized in the emerging post Civil War transition from the "coffin" to the "casket." The word for the latter, a rectangular case not tapered from the shoulder area as was the former, carried the connotation of a jewel box, a container for something valuable.

The pattern of increased investment of life, time, and resources in the dead may be seen also in the growth of an elaborate complex of funerary practice, stylized display of grief, and supporting death paraphernalia. While varying in degree with geographic locale and social strata, this complex included such matters as tightly defined periods of social mourning, precise strictures on the nature of dress, and carefully prescribed form in the use of a variety of items of death etiquette such as mourning cards, gloves, and crepe. The question here is not, of course, the worth of this practice, but merely the observation that as the century moved on, death and the dead, considerably groomed and polished from their rough appearance of earlier years, were allowed increasingly substantial demands on the lives of the living.

The suggested closure of life and death worlds had also a dimension far broader than changes in death ritual. Not only did death become a major theme in the popular culture of mid-nineteenth century America, but Americans in addition set out in large numbers to draw the afterlife more closely into the living world [2, 4]. Prior to the third decade of the nineteenth century very little attention was given to the exact nature of the afterlife. When speaking of that realm American ministers of the seventeenth and eighteenth centuries did so in vague terms gradually implying an alien and not particularly attractive landscape. Now as the nineteenth century progressed the public was encouraged by many of its religious leaders and a significant amount of popular literature to inquire into the most minute detail of heavenly existence, from how it looked to what, if anything, was eaten there. The end result was that the once awesome mystery of the spiritual world was reduced to a definition of a heavenly state much like that of life in middle class America at that time. The dead, who inhabited that realm, moreover, were perceived in the folk culture, if not theology, as never far away. They waited and watched the lives of the living with interest, both groups secure in their expectation of future reunion on life terms. As Ann Douglas has perceptively observed in her treatment of this subject, there was about all this a clear commitment to the denial of death as a separate state [4, p. 515]. Thus was the line between the world of the dead and that of the living significantly blurred.

The logical extreme of this merger of realms was the vogue of spiritualism, where actual communication occurred between dead world and living world. The movement reached peaks in the 1850s and again in the 1870s, and at one point could claim a million believers out of a national population of 25 million [5, p. 378]. Here was empirical support for the belief that the dead pass to a similar, though superior, state from their earthly condition. Here was proof that those dead wished to make themselves felt in earthly affairs and would assist if invited. Here was an unprecedented measure of interaction between two worlds very near indeed. The move from one to the other, that is, "passing on," could be almost just that — a matter of status change.

Dichotomizing Life and Death

The old accommodation of the nineteenth century has of course been dissolved. Americans no longer live their lives with the well-defined relationship to and interest in the dead world or with the acceptance of death as a natural part of life which characterized that period. Nor is the disappearance to be totally bemoaned. The nature of that association was in many ways restrictive on the living, naive, and premised upon the unhappy grim reality of a very high mortality rate. Death could hardly be denied, for example. There was too much of it around, particularly among the young. Even at the close of the century, life expectancy at birth was only forty-seven years, and infant mortality was approximately 162.4 per 1,000. Precisely when reversal of the closure began is difficult to establish, but it was clearly underway by the opening of the new century. The subsequent dichotomizing of living and dead worlds so apparent in contemporary America was a product of many factors. Among the most subtle, though drastic in consequences, have been the forces of urbanization, mobility, and demographic change which have caused death and the dead world to fade drastically from sight as well as in impact.

A number of scholars have spoken to the consequences of one or more of these factors, and it is therefore only necessary to note them briefly and to underscore their collective effect [6, Chapter 10, 7–9]. Mobility separated and subsequently acted to diminish emotional involvement or investment among family and relatives and among friends. After a period of separation even death meant less. The secondary and functionary personal relationships characteristic of the urban setting have meant that, in general, death would have much less personal impact than was the case in small close-knit communities of the past. City life encouraged also a bureaucratic solution to the problem of the dead as well as the dying, as it encouraged similar solutions to other social problems. Death and the dead became the province of the hospital and the funeral parlor rather than the home. Direct exposure to death was thereby minimized for many. Placed in the hands of institutional specialists where contact was routine, even impersonal, death and the dead came to interfere much less than ever before with the main stream of life.

Death has become much less visible also because increasingly it is the elderly who are doing the dying. This is a consequence of the drastic reduction in child and mid-life death in the present century. The elderly tend to be those members of the family least important functionally to its continuation. By the time their parents die, children of the elderly normally live apart from them and have established an immediate family of their own as the center of emotional investment. The elderly tend also to be in varying degree already disengaged from actual operation and ongoing life of the society. Death in this group, therefore, has the least effect on survivors as well as on the societal order. Social visibility of death and the dead is thus reduced. This consequence has been accelerated greatly in the past twenty years as a result of the extensive age-grading and isolation of the elderly via the retirement city/home movement. Moreover, death has become less visible in this century because it is less prevalent. The mortality rate in the United States has declined from 17.2 per 1,000 population in 1900 to a low of 9 per 1,000 in 1975. As Fulton has observed, increasing life expectancy and declining mortality rates have produced in contemporary America a "death-free" generation. For the first time in history a family may expect statistically to live twenty years without the passing of one of its members [8, p. 25]. In all such ways has death itself faded in visibility and impact, which in turn has made the maintenance of any sense of meaningful connection with those already gone all the more difficult.

But the dynamic and impersonal forces described above are not the whole story. Even more significant, though in many ways not unrelated, has been the growing temporal and secular outlook of this century. The case of the contemporary cemetery illustrates the point. It no longer functions as a bridge between the life and death worlds. That connection has been severed as the living have given up their commitment to continued communion with the dead. Part of the problem is that in a high-mobility rapidly-changing environment such as the United States maintaining a connection with a specific spot of earth is very difficult to do. Yet the popularity of now standardized operation and topography of the contemporary graveyard betrays also a significant shift in perspective on the dead world from that which produced the "rural cemetery" of the nineteenth century. The "perpetual care" concept has increasingly in this century released the living from any physical need to visit the gravesite. The cemetery itself has become almost totally depersonalized. The so-called Memorial Park movement which was under way as early as the 1920s began to substitute small ground-level bronze plaques for the ornate headstones of the nineteenth century. It also eliminated epitaphs and the traditional coffin-size "mound" — a constant reminder in earlier days of the reality of death. Only the random pieces of statuary and other adornment which characterize such "parks" betray the true nature of the site to passers by. The overall point is this: Americans now do not need nor want the association they once had with the deceased. The readily identifiable garden-park cemetery of the nineteenth century with its personalized gravesite expressive of the individual was designed to encourage relationship with the dead world and the dead. Current impersonality, particularly to the point of almost unmarked ground, points in the opposite direction.

A similar withdrawal from commitment to the dead is apparent in other forms of death ritual. Simple contrast with the late nineteenth century makes the case. Gone are the elaborate rules of social mourning which could dictate the conduct of a widow for up to a year. Also gone are the formal mourning costume and supporting paraphernalia of the past. As Kephart noted in his study of Philadelphia, only one of the once-standard mourning shops remained in that city by 1950 [10, p. 641]. The process of restricting the time and space given over to the dead would progress to the point where any expression of grief over loss became something to be avoided. The elaborate Victorian funeral began to fade in the World War I era; and, more significantly, present funerary ritual has been under heavy attack at least since the late 1950s. Such rites are said to be too time consuming, too disruptive of city traffic, too costly, too barbaric, and so forth.

Criticism of contemporary funerals may be justified, though it is worth noting here that only the anger directed at them is new. The aspects under attack have long been around and only recently have been defined as matters of extensive popular discontent. The gradual rejection of social mourning and elaborate funerary practice may also be quite natural consequences of other not-directly-related occurrences. Fulton has made the interesting point that a great deal of the feeling that the traditional funeral is inappropriate may be related to the fact that it is the elderly who largely do the dying now [8]. For earlier noted reasons deaths within this group tend to be "low-grief" affairs for survivors, and require only minimal acknowledgement of the passing for emotional closure. Anything else seems unwarranted. Presumably the same case could be made on other forms of ritual display. Specifically on the matter of the loss of social mourning custom, Sybil Wolfram finds the primary cause in the decline of the significance of kinship ties, a matter already apparent by the close of the nineteenth century [11]. Whatever the causes, however, the point is this: in the present century Americans have been reducing steadily the degree of time and resources they are willing to provide the dead.

Finally, and in larger perspective, the dead world has been largely lost because an increasingly temporal and secular-minded living world has actively chosen to abandon even the topic itself. Though hardly news, it should be noted here nonetheless that in this century death has become a taboo. Very little relationship is possible with a realm which we are rigorously seeking to forget. The cause of that taboo, as well as the general death-avoidance which characterizes American society in this century, has been a source of much recent scholarship. Fulton and Geis as well as Geoffrey Gorer have probably identified the most fundamental factor, however. In a culture which will support no longer the certainty of afterlife, natural death and physical decomposition have become too horrible to contemplate or discuss [12, p. 67-68, 13, p. 51].

The matter of the temporal-secular nature of contemporary American society suggests another observation. One way to soften the grim reality of death is to treat it as a great event, a beginning rather than an end. That vision has increasingly lost its force in this century. Indeed even within the present-day church, the reward for religious adherence is really no longer placed in a world beyond this one. Rather, it is offered in terms of quality of life in the here and now. Goldscheider contends that this particular change is related to the "mortality revolution" of this century [14, p. 187-188]. Perhaps that same phenomenon may help to explain also the loss of concern with the theme of natural death and its meaning which is apparent in American philosophy and literature in this century. The main point here, however, is that the disappearance of certainty about, as well as concern with, the afterlife has had profound implications for the relationship between the living world and dead world. Relationship becomes extremely difficult because the living literally do not know where the dead are. Without a fixed location, understandable in human terms, the deceased are truly lost.

The Consequences of Dichotomization

So for all practical purposes the dead world has been detached from the living world and is rapidly disappearing. Perhaps this development makes little difference. Perhaps in a more positive sense what has occurred should be understood as a progressive liberation for the living from a largely unhealthy earlier accommodation with the dead. Certainly the period of the old intertwine could not be taken as a "golden age" of relations between the two. And, indeed, if there is room to question the present state, it arises less from need to restore the old order than from the extreme nature of our present withdrawal from the dead. In brief, what does it mean to abandon the dead world, the end result of the course we have taken for some time? It is a matter worth serious consideration. A first comment on this subject is that we treat the dying badly. We avoid them, isolate them, and generally approach them as if their status were an embarrassment. Without attempting to establish which was cause and which was effect historically, I would observe simply that such treatment is not surprising in a culture which has allowed so much distance to develop between itself and the dead. A closer relationship might well involve a change in our treatment of those soon to enter that category.

Secondly, accepting one's own death is a difficult matter even under the best of circumstances, and the present American perspective on the dead world most probably increases that difficulty. Having made little place in life for the dead and having had little experience with even the subject of death, the individual can only perceive that event as totally alien, surely therefore all the more terrifying. Because natural death and the dead have come to play such a minimal role in the culture, that culture in turn can provide essentially no resources to the individual which might assist one in meeting one's own death or that of others. Indeed, the absence of contact with the dead world actively works to sustain in the culture a system of death denial which strongly discourages all effort toward acceptance.

Thirdly, much has been said in contemporary America about the need for self identity and the difficulties of establishing it. While the matter is complex, certainly one traditional dimension has been the understanding of a clear relationship, individually and collectively, to the generational stream past to future. The ability to do this has been significantly weakened in recent years, in part because of a general tendency toward ahistorical outlook. But most assuredly this difficulty has been aggravated also by our steady movement toward denying the dead world a role in the living world. This denial is after all a rejection of both our past and future. If the dead are simply gone and irrelevant as those presently alive are soon to be, the chain of historical continuity is broken at every link. We are the worse for the loss of this aspect of identity.

Fourth, we have gone a very long way toward eliminating the presence of the dead world from life but death does come, and in the end our vision of it has a way of also informing our view of life. Because the dead world is largely understood as irrelevant to our lives, death tends to become without significance and absurd. Because we have this perspective on the end of life, it becomes difficult to avoid the same view on all of life. A greater willingness to admit the dead into the living world could be a very significant step in releasing us from our current philosophical bankruptcy before death.

Finally, and assuming a closer association with the dead would have value, there is the question of whether recovery of relationship is possible in today's temporal, secular, and youth oriented culture where so many forces seem to work against it. The theoretical answer to the question at least, is yes. The difficulty to be overcome is less one of developing specific connections (though such efforts are worthwhile) than one of obtaining popular recognition that the dead world should be a concern of the living. The return of the dead to a place in our literature, philosophy, and theology could be a good beginning. Perhaps, indeed some start has been made, for death and bereavement have found their way into a place of significant concern among social scientists recently. One scholar has observed that more material appeared on this subject in the five years following the publication of Herman Feifel's seminal work, *The Meaning of Death* (1959), than had appeared in the previous hundred years [8, p. 24]. As witnessed in the recent work of Elisabeth Kubler-Ross and others, there is even renewed interest in the question of existence beyond clinical death.

The great value of this new scholarly concern for the dead world is twofold. One is the assistance it provides in making death a respectable topic for discussion again, a necessary step before any serious reconsideration of relationship with the dead. The second is that sensitive examination into the needs of the dying and those left behind, which is a major thrust of the new literature, is intimately related to the matter of the role of the dead among the living. Popular reception of the former should almost automatically help create a climate favorable to exploration of the latter. There is therefore some reason for optimism that in time the dead can be reintegrated in a meaningful way into the living world. There is beyond that, much more reason to believe that the effort should be made.

REFERENCES

1. C. Covey, *The American Pilgrimage: The Roots of American Religion and Culture,* Peter Smith, New York, 1961.
2. L. Saum, Death in the Popular Mind of Pre-Civil War America, In: David Stannard (ed.), *Death in America,* University of Pennsylvania Press, Philadelphia, pp. 30-48, 1975.
3. R. Habenstein and W. Lamers, *The History of American Funeral Directing,* Bulfin Printers, Milwaukee, 1955.
4. A. Douglas, Heaven Our Home: Consolation Literature in the Northern United States 1830-80, David Stannard (ed.), *Death in America,* University of Pennsylvania Press, Philadelphia, pp. 49-68, 1975.
5. E. D. Branch, *The Sentimental Years, 1836-1860,* Hill and Wang, New York, 1934.
6. L. Bowman, *The American Funeral: A Study in Guilt, Extravagance, and Sublimity,* Public Affairs Press, Washington, D. C., 1959.
7. R. Blauner, Death and Social Structure, *Psychiatry: Journal for the Study of Interpersonal Processes,* pp. 29, 378-94, 1966.
8. R. Fulton, Death, Grief and Social Recuperation, *Omega, 1:*1, pp. 23-28, 1970.
9. R. Kalish, The Effects of Death Upon the Family, Leonard Pearson (ed.), *Death and Dying: Current Issues in the Treatment of the Dying Person,* Case Western, Cleveland, pp. 79-107, 1969.
10. W. Kephart, Status After Death, *American Sociological Review, 15,* pp. 635-43, 1950.
11. S. Wolfram, The Decline of Mourning, *The Listener, 75,* pp. 763-64, 1966.
12. R. Fulton and G. Geis, Death and Social Values, Robert Fulton (ed.), *Death and Identity,* John Wiley, New York, pp. 67-75, 1965.
13. G. Gorer, The Pornography of Death, *Encounter, 5,* pp. 49-52, 1955.
14. C. Goldscheider, The Mortality Revolution, Edwin Shneidman (ed.), *Death: Current Perspectives,* Mayfield Publishing Co., Palo Alto, Calif., pp. 163-88, 1976.

The Days of the Dead in Oaxaca, Mexico: An Historical Inquiry

Judith Strupp Green

Dias de Todos Muertos, or Days of the Dead, is the collective name by which the Catholic holydays of All Saints' on November first and All Souls' on November second are known in Mexico. The unique flavor of the celebration of these universal Catholic festivals in some traditional Indian communities and in Indian sections of larger cities has long been recognized. The Island of Janitzio in Michoacán and Zapotec villages in the Valley of Oaxaca are two such areas.

Among those raised in the Western heritage of death-avoidance, the observation of the Days of the Dead in traditional parts of Mexico often elicits a reaction of mild shock and even repulsion. Death iconography mingled with gustatory delights (sugar skulls, coffin candies), toys for children (skeleton puppets), and politics (the calaveras news-sheet) and the ordinary pursuits of the living grates against contemporary North American and European attitudes towards death. Certain customs carried out in graveyards on these days or nights, such as gambling or playing board games on the tombstones, or eating a picnic lunch there, have the same effect. Although these customs are actually peripheral rather than central to the ritual itself, they are consonant with the ancient indigenous beliefs about the dead.

Below the surface of cursory examination, the Days of the Dead are revealed as a result of the amalgamation of pre-Spanish Indian ritual and belief and the imposed ritual and dogma of the Spanish Catholic Church. This study attempts to illuminate some elements of the historical and cultural backdrop to the contemporary celebration of the Dias de Todos Muertos in a traditional area—the Valley of Oaxaca.

Ethnographic data for the description of the Days of the Dead were gathered during two trips to the Valley of Oaxaca in 1963 and 1966. Two markets, that of Oaxaca City and Tlacolula, eleven homes in eight Zapotec villages in the valley, and three cemeteries were visited at least once during this time and photographs taken. The process of making the bread of the dead (*pan de los muertos*), a ubiquitous and important artifact in connection with these holydays, was observed and recorded at one home bakery in Oaxaca, less intensively in two others. The sequence of ritual outlined here was given by Sra. Soledad Ramirez, a Zapotec woman of the Barrio de Xochimilco in Oaxaca. Her mother, who lived with her, commented on older customs and checked her daughter's information.

Collectively, the Days of the Dead are one of the most important festivals in Oaxaca and certainly one of the most expensive for each family. About a month before the Days of the Dead the women of the family begin to buy and store up material for the altar and the dishes and ollas for the preparation and serving of foods, according to Sra. Ramirez. She indicated that the purchase of all new dishes was mandatory, to please the spirits, no matter how poor any family might be.

On the thirty-first of October, Allhallows Eve, the family stays up all night. Food for the altar and for guests is prepared—including chiles, black and red *moles*, and tamales. Greatest importance is given to the preparation of tamales. When the laborious work of making them is over and they are thrown into the *ollas* to steam, boys set off firecrackers in celebration.

The altar in the home is also arrayed on that night. Either a special table is set up or the family altar, if it is large enough, is used. Sra. Ramirez stated that formerly, while living in a more spacious house, they put up both an altar for the child dead as well as that for adults. It had everything that the adult altar had in miniature, including tiny candleholders, small fruits and vegetables, and toys. Only "adult" foods, tobacco and alcohol, were omitted. An altar fitting this description was later seen at Santa Lucia del Valle. As well as being considered an altar to the child dead, it was designated as the special altar of the living child of the household.

The children's spirits arrive at 4:00 a.m. on November first, according to Sra. Ramirez. They are called *angelitos*. One tiny candle is lit at this time for each child. At 8:00 a.m. the same morning the child spirits are said to leave, and the little candles are snuffed and removed from the main altar. A mass is said in the local church on the morning of the first.

The adult spirits arrive on the afternoon of the same day, at 3:00 p.m., at which time a candle of standard size is lit for each. At 8:00 p.m. that evening the family says the rosary. No one would eat anything laid out on the altar for fear of antagonizing the spirits of the dead. Sra. Ramirez expressed the belief that the angry ghosts would tie their feet up in the night if they ate from the altar. Leaving nothing (or inferior gifts) on the altar causes the spirits to be sad and/or angry, depending on the folktale quoted. Usually however, the dead are believed to take revenge for poor treatment on this day.

The next morning, November second, is All Souls' Day; three masses are said and at 8:00 a.m. the adult spirits leave. Responses for the dead go on all day in various cemeteries in the Valley. Priests or prayer leaders bless and sprinkle the graves with holy water and say prayers for the dead. This goes on for many days after the Days of the Dead have passed, in order to reach all the cemeteries.

The evening of the second, about sundown, people in villages where the responses will be said decorate the graves in the cemetery with flowers, candles, and incense. Children's graves receive the most elaborate treatment, including tiny candles, ollas and miniature gourds, toys and cardboard or plaster figures, representing the dead or the afterlife.

It is this afternoon and evening, too, when relatives and friends come to visit, pray at the altar, and offer a gift to the souls. The gift is referred to as a *muerto*, and consists mainly of foods selected from those on the altar and prepared specially for the day. Guests, in return, receive food from their hosts. Hot beaten chocolate and bread of the dead were given to a Zapotec woman guest, during our visit to a home in Teotitlan on the second. She was a *comadre* (ritual co-godparent) to the family. Formerly, stated the mother of Sra. Ramirez, groups of men came to the houses in costumes and masks and sang special hymns of praise, *alabanzas*, for the dead and received gifts of fruits and altar goods. Until about two years ago they came, unmasked, to pray and sing and ask "Hay muertos?" (are there any *muertos* or gifts?), but the custom has apparently died out in the barrio. In the 1930's Parsons mentions masked men on domiciliary begging trips on the Days of the Dead at Santo Domingo Alvarrados and San Baltazar, Zapotec towns in the Valley (Parsons 1936: 282-283).

At Xochimilco Barrio the Days of the Dead are officially over on November third. The altars are not dismantled there until the fourth of November, however. Food on the altars can be eaten as soon as the spirits leave on the morning of the second, and it is used as the source of supply for the *muertos* gifts.

Informants at Santiago Ixtaltepec and Teotitlan offered different time-tables for the coming and going of the spirits, though all agreed that the child ghosts came on the 1st and the adults arrived on the first and left on the second.

RITUAL OBJECTS ASSOCIATED WITH THE DAYS OF THE DEAD

Associated with the Days of the Dead are: unmodified natural objects, man-made objects not directly representational of death or dying, and man-made artifacts directly representing death themes.

1. Altar at Mitla, Oaxaca

2. Altar in the Valley of Oaxca

In the first two categories of non-representational objects associated with these festival days are included much of the altar contents and grave decorations. Altars examined and inventoried in the villages had in common these elements: fruits and vegetables, dishes, candles or vigil lights, chocolate, semposuchil (*Tagetes*) which is a flower resembling the marigold and at least one other variety of flower, often coxcomb or a wild flower (*Stevia*), or paper flowers (Fig 1, 2). Bread of the dead was always on the altar, as were religious prints. Figures with macabre themes were seen on only two altars. These figures were, however, used in the traditional cemetery.

Objects found on several altars were baskets, lacquered gourd bowls, embroidered cloths and incense burners. Two canes bent to form an arch behind the altar were common to some homes, as was the practice of setting the new dishes in a cylindrical wickerwork basket under the altar.

Aside from altar decorations, other material associated with the Days of the Dead are the gifts or *muertos*, brought to relatives and *compadres*. A *muerto* consists of items from the altar, as well as foodstuffs specially prepared for the holydays. An earthenware jar of black *mole*, or a cup of chocolate, fruits, flowers, nuts, tortillas wrapped in napkins and carried in a basket, along with a candle are typical.

Other special foods for the Days of the Dead are tamales and a sweet food made of squash, *conserva de calabaza*. The bread of the dead, *pan de los muertos*, is apparently indispensable for the celebration of these days in the Valley. Special loaves are prepared by bakers from the villages. Even the local commercial bakery in Oaxaca City brings in young men from Santo Domingo Comaltepec, "the village of the master bakers," for the occasion, solely to bake massive quantities of these loaves. The Indian bakers in the small barrios use old-fashioned brick beehive ovens to make three classes of bread of the dead, classed according to the amount of egg and types of spices used. There are minor differences in the shape and decoration of the loaves within the Valley—the baker from a Oaxaca barrio, who was originally from Ixtlan de Juarez, and those from Sto. Domingo Comaltepec fashioned them in an oval shape with a small knob at one end. On this knob was pressed a painted face or winged angel molded of white dough (Fig 3). In Tlacolula the larger loaves were sprinkled with hearts and crosses made of beaten egg white and

3. Bread of the Dead in preparation, Oaxaca, Oaxaca.

colored sugar. A baker from Etla fashioned ghostly, human-looking figures with orange bean eyes.

No food is offered on the graves, although people sometimes eat their lunch in the cemetery while visiting graves, or bring bread of the dead and other food as an offering to those saying the responses, as at Santiago Ixtaltepec. Each loaf of bread represents a soul, according to informants.

Other representational artifacts include symbols of funerary equipment such as tombs, coffins, and pallbearers (Fig. 4). Symbols of the afterlife include angels, devils, lyres, the soul in purgatory consumed in flames and the disembodied heart. These artifacts are made in sugar, clay, plaster, paper-mache and cardboard. They may be static figures or puppets (Fig 5, 6). Many depict skeletal figures engaged in everyday, or comical activities—such as laughing skeleton puppets, plaster skeletons dressed as bishops, women with babies, priests, scholars, etc. The sugar ones are edible, and those made in Etla and brought to Oaxaca from that town, which is known for its fine candies, are filled with anise flavored liqueur. Tiny pottery fruits and miniature dishes are set out on children's

4. Market stand in Oaxaca City with funeral figures for home altars.

5. Sugar skull from Oaxaca City.

graves. In areas other than Oaxaca (i.e. Michoacán, Edo de Mexico, Guanajuato) more emphasis is concentrated on molded animal figures, especially in sugar.

Grave decorations consist of flowers, candles or vigil lights, and, on occasion, representational figurines, especially cardboard tombs (*tumbitas*) or paper skulls. Occasionally those visiting the graves would set out an incense burner before the cross or headstone. These examples are drawn from the graves seen at the San Felipe del Agua cemetery and that at Santiago Ixtaltepec, both small traditional ones. The larger cemetery at San Antonino Castillo de Velasco (Fig 7) was only embellished with flower decorations, as was the main cemetery at Oaxaca City.

Another artifact connected with the cemetery ritual, at least at San Felipe, is the board game played by children on the unadorned gravestones. *El Ancla* and *La Oca* are both games played at other times of the year but, according to informants, are traditional for the Days of the Dead. Grown men played ordinary dice in the Santiago Ixtaltepec cemetery on the night the graves were blessed.

The *calaveras*, satirical verses written to lampoon local politicians and prominent

6. Skeleton puppet of Don Juan Tenorio, protagonist of the famous drama performed
   on the Days of the Dead.

persons, are printed on newssheets decorated with drawings of skeletons and distributed
during the Days of the Dead. The church bells are tolled in distinctive ways. Parsons
reports that at Mitla the bells ring double quick at noon on Oct. 31, as they do for
children's funerals. At noon on Nov. 2 they tolled as at an adult's funeral (1936:
281-282).

OFFICIAL CATHOLIC POSITION AND CUSTOMS SANCTIONED BY THE CHURCH

The Days of the Dead are official holydays in the Catholic Calendar. November first
was established in 834 A. D. as All Saints' Day by Pope Gregory IV as a day to honor all
the saints, including the unrecognized as well as the canonized saints who had attained
the Beatific Vision (New Catholic Encyc. 1967: Vol. 1, 318-319). It coincided with the
ancient festival to Samhain, Celtic Lord of the Dead, at which human and animal
sacrifices were made.

The day following All Saints' is All Souls' Day, established in the Roman calendar by
the fourteenth century, following its institution as a day of observance in the Cluniac

7. Decorated grave at the cemetary at San Antonino Castillo de Velasco.

monasteries by Odilo, Abbot of Cluny, France in the ninth century. It was founded to honor all the faithful departed, and on it the Office of the Dead and three Requiem Masses are said by the clergy to assist the souls from purgatory to heaven.

The custom of having a procession from the church to the cemetery, visiting the graves of deceased relatives and friends, the blessing of the graves by a priest, and decorating the graves with flowers and candles is almost universal in Catholic countries (New Catholic Encyc. 1967: Vol. 1, 319) and looked upon with favor by the Church (Weiser 1952: 308-311).

The color of vestments and altar drapings on the Days of All Souls' is black, according to Catholic liturgy. In some churches in New Spain, it was the custom of the clergy to erect a temporary catafalque in the church to remind the congregation of the purpose of the day, like the one that Pfefferkorn saw on All Souls' in a church in Sonora in the eighteenth century (Pfefferkorn 1949: 270). They also exhibited the relics of saints, often bones or skulls, on that day, as Felipe el Hermoso saw in the Cologne cathedral on November 1, 1501 (Lalaing in Garcia Mercadal 1952-1962: Vol. 1, 543). In Yucatan in the 1850's John Lloyd Stephens found that the skulls of former local residents were exposed on All Souls' Day on a catafalque at the church. He said this practice was general "all over the country". Each skull was identified by name on a strip of paper spanning the forehead (Stephens 1856: Vol. I, 420).

The Catholic Church promised heavenly rewards for those who died in the Faith and in the state of grace, pending a period of time in purgatorial flames for those who had not expiated their sins on earth, and eternal suffering in hell for those who did not die in the state of grace. The idea of purgatory was a concept that came into prominence in the High Middle Ages, for previously "the poets and theologians had been satisfied to leave the riddle of the soul's fate between death and final judgment unanswered" (Gatch 1969: 111). While theologically the idea of purgatory was accepted, the ordinary people evidently clung to some pre-Christian customs like feeding the dead which was carried over through early Christian and early Medieval times.

FOLK CUSTOMS IN MEDIEVAL TIMES

The pre-Christian practice of feeding the dead hinges on the belief that, for some time at least, the dead person continues to have needs like those of the living. The belief was apparently quite tenacious in Europe. In the fifteenth century the custom of laying out a banquet for dead family members on All Souls' Day was prevalent enough to receive an official ban by the Church in the fifteenth century. Hoyos Sainz, the Spanish folklorist, states that formerly in the Cantabrian zone of Spain, food was put into the tombs of the dead at burial, and on the night of All Saints an array of food was set in the windows as an offering for the dead (Hoyos Sainz 1945: 30-53). These practices are unknown today.

A common custom involving food with All Souls' Day was that of "souling", as it was called in Medieval England. Black-garbed friars walked through the streets ringing a bell and calling on the living to remember the dead in their prayers, while the soulers, often young men, sung verses called souling songs and begged alms and soul-cakes—square buns topped with currants.

Spain was a country so enamoured of death during the reign of the Hapsburgs (1516-1700) that one scholar was provoked to say "The Hapsburg attitude toward death was ... in accordance with the ethical temper of their subjects, if the evidence of our series of texts is valid. The Death tradition had invaded all walks of Spanish society" (Whyte 1931: 127). Charles V retired to a monastery and ordered his own funeral to be celebrated before his death. Philip II habitually dressed in black, as did his followers; he built the remarkable Escorial which has been described as a vast mausoleum. The Dance of Death composed in Spain ca. 1450 was performed during the fifteenth and sixteenth centuries as an allegorical and devotional dance (Whyte 1931: 20, 43). Religious poems and plays about death such as "La Farsa de la Muerte", "Las Cortes de la Muerte" and "La Vida y la Muerte" were evidently popular (Whyte 1931: 75, 100, 117).

Spanish devotion to the dead was so great as to amount to a death cult, according to the versions of it given by seventeenth and eighteenth century travelers to Spain. A Jourvin who journeyed to Spain in 1672 remarks that prayers were solicited for the dead continuously in all the churches, on the public plazas, and at all crossroads. At 9:00 p.m. the church bell rang to remind people to pray for the souls in purgatory, and men wandered the streets begging alms for the souls (Jourvin in Garcia Mercadal 1952: Vol. 2, 750). Pfefferkorn attests to the same practice, carried out by Spanish religious brotherhoods in Sonora, Mexico in 1756-1767 (Pfefferkorn 1949: 271-272).

During the Days of the Dead devotion was intensified. Juan F. Peyron, a traveler in

Spain in 1772-1773 remarks that "The love of the souls is universal in Spain; they even know the precise day when a soul ought to leave purgatory and often announce at the door of the church that 'today the soul is taken out' " (Peyron in Mercadal 1952: Vol. 3, 880). The same author reports that on the night before the "Dia de los Muertos," nearly all the Spanish towns and cities had a public auction to which people were expected to donate livestock and poultry or foodstuffs to be sold for the benefit of the souls. Dances and hunts were given to raise money to have masses said for the souls as well. On the day of All Saints', the people carried lighted candles to the tombs of their relatives because they believed that, in the evening before All Souls', the dead held a procession, and those for whom no one had taken a candle for the grave, attended ashamedly with their arms crossed. Some people even adorned their beds that night and left them empty, so that the wandering souls could rest (Peyron in Mercadal 1952: Vol. 3, 880-881).

Hoyos Sainz, the Spanish folklorist, states that in this century the custom of giving bread of the souls (*pan de animas* and *pan de muertos*) to beggars on the Days of the Dead was still practiced in Leon, Salamanca, and Segovia (Hoyos Sainz 1945: 30-53). The Catholic Church was able to stamp out the practice of feeding the dead in Spain, possibly encouraging the giving of food and alms to the poor or to the Church to benefit the souls (i.e. the public auction). Although it was practiced in earlier times, the Catholic Church would not have introduced or encouraged this pre-Christian rite. The ritual they brought to the New World is generally considered to be a reduced and expurgated one. As Foster states " . . . in missionizing America the Church had the opportunity to throw off these popular observances, to define Catholicism in terms of rites and observances central to dogma, to produce a theologically ideal religion" (Foster 1960: 15). The fact that they did not always take this opportunity in America, especially when the popular custom worked to the benefit of the Church—such as the giving of bread of the dead and begging alms for the souls—is apparent from the older and contemporary accounts of the Days of the Dead ritual in Mexico. Also they were faced with the New World indigenous tradition of honoring and sustaining souls by feeding them—the same custom that existed in rural Europe.

ICONOGRAPHY OF THE DEAD AND OF DEATH IN MEDIEVAL EUROPE

The obsessive concern with death and the dead found in Spain has its roots in the dominance of death themes in literature and art in most of Europe in the late Middle Ages. This trend has precedents in the thirteenth and fourteenth centuries with the theme of the *Three Living and Three Dead*, the *Art of Dying Well* and finally culminated in the *Dance of Death*. Macabre paintings inspired by these themes appear in and on Medieval European structures. One exception is Spain, which had its own *Danza de la Muerte*, but no painted representations of it have been found. The morbid spirit lasted longer in Spain than in the rest of Europe, through the Hapsburg reign. Trapier (1956: 31) feels that death themes in the forms of skulls or skeletons are more frequent in the funerary art of the seventeenth century than during the previous century, not to mention the influence of the lugubrious works of Valdes Leal.

Kurtz poses his belief that the instigation and promotion of the death theme should be attributed to the Medieval clergy who, concerned about the general decay of morals at the time, and the loss of value put on life because of devastating outbreaks of the Black Death, felt people needed the grim reminder that the sinner's life was short and that he had to repent in time to save himself (Kurtz 1934: 281). The Dominicans, so dominant in the missionization of Mexico, were cited as particularly instrumental in this movement (Whyte 1931: 13).

Vivid visual images were used to convey the idea of Death and the dead. Men dressed in painted skeleton suits acted in the *autos*, as they no doubt did for the Dance of the Dead. Cheap, popular woodcuts and the ubiquitous paintings and murals of death themes depicted the dead as near-skeletons, that is, as partly dessicated corpses. These were not always gruesome. The famous woodcuts of Holbein on death, which were available by 1555 in Spain, showed "death [as] an abstract, personified concept that enters into the daily life of the people of the world and mingles with them like another human being" (Kurtz 1934: 194). The dead in his graphics appear in contemporary clothing and indulge in practical jokes on the living. This familiar, tongue-in-cheek characterization of death was to reappear in the nineteenth century graphics of Mexican artists José Guadalupe Posada, Manuel Manilla and Santiago Hernández, as the famous skeletons known as *calaveras*.

In addition to graphics, the death motif appeared on sepulchral monuments, catafalques, architectural ornaments and jewelry, both religious and secular. These reminders of death are called *memento mori*. "What may be termed the memento mori age included the fifteenth, sixteenth, and seventeenth centuries, and the popularity of memento mori devices certainly culminated in the 'Dance of Death' designs of the sixteenth century ... memento mori devices occurred everywhere, on paintings, and prints, on sepulchral monuments, as architectural ornaments, on all kinds of jewelry (especially on memorial finger rings), in books of emblems, in books of hours and other kinds of devotional books, on devotional objects (such as rosary beads in the form of death's heads) and on medals[11] (Weber 1922: 135-136). The catafalque for Carlos V in Mexico was covered with skeletons called "muertes" (Cervantes Salazar 1963: 188-200). The catalfalque designed for Carlos II in Coatepec, Puebla, in 1700 was similarly adorned.

Actual skulls and skeletons were not uncommon sights to the Medieval and Renaissance man. Charnel houses were integral parts of the popular cemeteries, where the bones of earlier deceased were heaped up after being exhumed to make room for others who wished to be buried there. Public executions and exposure of the victims' bodies or heads for extended periods were common practice. Parts of the bodies of saints, including hair, nails, but particularly the skull and various bones, were venerated as relics and regularly exposed in the Churches (Huizinga 1924: 150).

AZTEC RITUAL FOR THE DEAD

Much more is known of pre-Columbian Aztec ritual, iconography, and eschatology than any other Mesoamerican group, thanks to the work of Sahagún and later investigators like Caso, Seler, Fernández, Angel María Garibay and León-Portilla. There may have been significant differences between their ritual and outlook and that of the pre-Columbian Zapotecs who occupied the Valley of Oaxaca. Aztec customs and beliefs as well as place names and vocabulary were known to have influenced the Zapotecs, however, after their invasion by the Aztec peoples in the fifteenth century, and previously through trade contacts (Parsons 1936: 2).

The Aztecs believed in an afterlife, though not an infinite one. The attainment of this afterlife did not hinge on the morality of one's behavior in life, except in the way that it might influence the manner of death. The way in which one died was considered a calling by a god. Those who went to the dwelling place of the sun (*Tonatiuhilhuicac*) were those who died in battle or on the sacrificial stone, and the women who died with a "prisoner in the womb" (in childbirth). Even this fate lasted only four years when they turned into various types of birds of rich plumage and color and would sip the honey of all the flowers of heaven and earth, according to Sahagún (1952: Bk. 3, 34-48).

Tlalocán, the earthly paradise, was the destined home of those chosen by Tlaloc, the god of rain. They died by drowning, lightning, dropsy or gout, which was considered the summons of the god. There is some evidence that after four years they were considered to be reborn on earth (León-Portilla 1963: 125-127). Those who died a natural death had a less pleasant fate. They had to make an arduous journey to Mictlan, the underworld, accompanied only by the little dog cremated with them, and face a series of tests, among them: trekking through eight deserts and eight hills, facing wild animals and obsidian-bladed winds. After four years they came to the ninth hill called Chiconamictlan and passed into nothingness (Sahagún 1952: Bk. 3, 39-42).

Both Parsons and Leslie, in their studies of the Zapotecs of Mitla, confirm that the villagers retain some of the fatalistic view towards death and the afterlife that was prevalent at the time of the Conquest. Despite over 400 years of missionary effort, heaven and hell in the Christian sense of reward for good or punishment for evil in this life was not accepted. *Gabihl*, the "hell" of the Zapotecs, "designated a realm of the dead coexistent with this world in which the souls lived much as they lived during this lifetime . . . Similarly, townspeople did not conceive of heaven as a dwelling place of the souls. It was for them a vague, far-away place where God and some saints lived" (Leslie 1960: 49-50). Nor was the idea of purgatory internalized. "The soul of a person who died abruptly because an *alma en pena*, an afflicted soul that could not complete its transition to the other world. This idea did not, however, conform to the Catholic conception of purgatory. The soul experiencing the *pena,* pain, consequent to sudden death was not atoning for sin; it was simply harrassed by the compulsion to complete the expectations and obligations that death had interrupted" (Leslie 1960: 48-49).

In pre-Hispanic times the Aztecs cremated those who died naturally. The remaining bones and ashes were placed in a jar or bowl, and upon them a green stone or lump of obsidian was laid to serve as the dead man's heart.in the other world. The ash-filled bowl was buried in the home or in the tribal temple, and offerings were laid on that spot (Sahagún Bk III: 43).

Although Sahagún does not specify that these first offerings were burned, or of what they consisted, Torquemada states that for a chief the gifts were slaves, quail, rabbits, birds, butterflies, incense, food wine, flowers, and canes of tobacco. At the end of a year slaves were no longer offered, but other gifts of food, flowers and incense were, accompanied with music, feasting and dancing (Torquemada 1943: Bk XIII, 521-523). Eighty days after death, says Sahagún in recounting ritual for those who died naturally, gifts and belongings were burned, and again in one year, and on the second, third and fourth anniversaries of death. After the fourth year all offerings stopped as the dead had reached their end.

The dead who went to one of the heavens, however, were honored at fixed festivals. Those who had been taken by Tlaloc to Tlalocan were feted at the feast of Tepeihuitl in the thirteenth month. Images were made of amaranth dough in the shape of clouds and human figures, which Torquemada likened to dolls, and were offered to the gods along with tamales and other food. Later they were eaten by the people (Sahagún 1951: Bk II, 121-123). In addition the people drank wine and uttered canticles of praise in honor of these dead holy ones.

On Quecholli in the fourteenth month, they observed a feast which honored the dead warriors by placing small arrows and torches on their graves and performing nighttime rites. The women who died in childbirth, the Cihuapipiltin, were also honored on the third movable feast in the third sign in the first house. Offerings were made to them, and these women, now goddesses, were thought to visit the earth on that day (Sahagún 1951: Bk II, 36).

Dr. Jacinto de la Serna noted in his *Tratado de las Idolatrías, Supersticiones, Dioses, Ritos, Hechiceríasy Otras Costumbres Gentilicas de las Razas Aborigenes de México,* first published in 1546, that the Indians adulterated Church custom by making offerings to the dead in their homes and burning candles to them there all night before All Souls'. In the churches that were not attended that night by priests they did the same, offering the dead good food and drink and later eating it themselves. On the day of All Souls' when the mass is said, he complains, the Indians had no more candles, since they had burned them the night before (de la Serna 1953: 69). He named as idolatrous their customs of offering food and drink to the dead, placing provisions in the shroud for the journey to the other life, and dressing them in new and fine clothing. When a baby died, its mother put a small cane, filled with her milk, on its breast for sustenance (de la Serna 1953: 68).

Burgoa, in his seventeenth century account of Zapotec life, laments the fact that the Indians continued to hold "superstitious banquets" for dead relatives and friends, sacrificing turkeys and preparing strong drink for the guests and singers (Burgoa 1934: Vol. 1, 22).

AZTEC ICONOGRAPHY OF THE DEAD AND OF DEATH

The actual remains of the dead were a familiar sight to the Aztecs, despite the cremation custom, for human sacrifices accompanied almost every festival. At the dedication of the Great Temple at Tenochtitlan about 20,000 captives were sacrificed. The skulls were sometimes spitted on racks known as *tzompantli*, and the skins of victims were worn by the priests for certain observances.

The custom of venerating parts of the bodies of the dead, especially those dead considered to have gone to paradise, was prevalent and undoubtedly aided the clergy in spreading belief in the efficacy of saintly relics after the conquest. Trophy heads of important war victims, dried and preserved, were kept, and there is evidence of a jawbone cult in Tlatelolco (Ruz 1968: 201). The arms, hands, and middle finger of women who died in childbirth were much sought after by young warriors as a source of supernatural power. So great was their value, that the family of the dead woman had to guard her grave for some time after death.

Although death motifs may have reached their apogee in Aztec art, symbols of death in the forms of skull and skeleton, corpse, or the perhaps characteristically Mesoamerican representation of a human that is vertically divided into skeleton and living person, appear from pre-Classic times through the Classic and post-Classic in all the important civilizations of Mesoamerica. The death's-head was the symbol of a particular month in one of the Aztec calendars, which was derived in turn from the Maya.

Although the fragile materials such as wood and cloth are gone, the death themes have been found in painting, sculpture, architectural ornament, pottery figurines, and jewelry.

Obviously the symbol of death to the Aztecs was not an admonition to reform since the forces controlling an individual's destiny were superhuman and his fate was established irrevocably at birth. Westheim feels that the Aztec *calavera* (skull) was an allusion to immortality and a sign of coming resurrection (1953: 54). But if life after death was a mere four years, and that fraught with danger and trial for the ordinary man, it is doubtful if it could mean that to the Aztec individual. Perhaps it was a device used by the religious hierarchy to keep the idea of the necessity of death—human sacrifice—before the people, since it was the only means by which the Aztecs believed they could avoid the destruction of their world by the gods (León-Portilla 1963: 36-37).

SUMMARY

The outward form of ritual prescribed for the Catholic Church for the Days of the Dead are: the obligatory mass on All Saints' Day, the celebration of three masses on All Souls' Day (a custom established by the Spanish Dominicans in the fifteenth century), and the recitation of the Office of the Dead. Common customs established by the Church in Europe such as the parish procession to the cemetery, the blessing of the graves, and the decoration by the people of relatives' tombstones with flowers and candles were no doubt introduced by the friars into Mexico, recognizing that placing offerings at the place of burial was already an Aztec custom.

Certain aspects of the Spanish death cult reached the New World, such as the custom of forming religious brotherhoods whose members solicited alms for the dead, ringing bells in special ways for the dead, and possibly erecting catafalques and exposing human skulls in the churches. The custom of begging for the souls in Spain obviously relates to the singing and soliciting alms at homes in Oaxaca on All Saints'. The meaning this ritual had to the Zapotec Indians as opposed to the meaning it had to the Spanish settlers may be quite different, however.

Related to this is the old Spanish tradition of giving visitors bread of the souls or bread of the dead. Noting that bread is listed among the death-offerings that the Indians brought to the church, in the sixteenth century by Motolinía (1951: 144-145), and in the early seventeenth century by Thomas Gage (Thompson 1958: 238-239), it is very possible that bread of the dead as part of the Days of the Dead ritual was introduced early in the Colonial period. Although the Aztecs did make figures of amaranth to offer to the dead and this custom may have been influential in the custom's acceptance, the purely Spanish technology of the bread-making and identical term used in Spain for it suggests that it was an Hispanic introduction.

The iconography of death for the Days of the Dead shows Spanish elements in the catafalque, coffin, and symbols of the afterlife such as the lyre, angels, valentine-type hearts, devils and souls in purgatory. Black and purple, used on these days for decoration, are the colors used in the Catholic liturgy for death and penance. To my knowledge the dessicated corpse or skin-and-bones figure does not appear in the Mesoamerican death iconography, but the skeleton itself, of course, does.

Many of the elements of ritual and iconography in the Oaxacan version of the Days of the Dead are syncretic. That is, they are the result of a process of integration of both Spanish and Indian traits during the missionization period and later. The Mesoamerican Indians honored and made offerings to their dead. The Spanish did too, but when they attempted to impose Catholic ritual on the Indians, they found that their converts sometimes changed the form to better fit with their own pre-Hispanic ritual and belief. When they accepted the form, they imbued it with a meaning more consistent with their own body of beliefs. Some of the acceptance or rejection patterns depended on the Spanish friars' tolerance, of course. The feeding of the dead, deplored by de la Serna and Burgoa, apparently was tolerated in the New World as it was in Spain as a superstition rather than idolatry or heresy. The Indians' all-night vigil awaiting the visit of the dead falls into the same category.

Symbols of death in the form of sugar skulls and animals have been documented only to the 1840's when Madam Calderon de la Barca reported the rows of sugar skulls and animals in the zocalo in Mexico City before All Saints' (1966: 541-542).

These ephemeral objects, along with the cardboard catafalques, seem to be replacements for the real skulls, sacrificial animals and catafalques once part of the Days of the Dead observance. The transference of death themes to toys and candies for children is entirely consonant with ancient and modern Indian beliefs regarding childhood participation in religious ritual. And there is no need to hide the facts of death from the Indian child. It is an event with which he is intimately familiar, not only because of the depressingly high mortality rate, but because death, like birth, takes place in the home and with the family.

REFERENCES

Burgoa, F. Geográfica descripción de la parte septentrional del polo artico de la América, y nueva iglesia de las indias occidentales. Mexico: Talleres Gráficos de la Nación, 1934.

Calderón de la Barca, F. In H. T. Fisher and M. H. Fisher (Eds.), Life in Mexico. The letters of Fanny Calerón de la Barca. Garden City, New York: Doubleday, 1966.

Catholic University of America. The new Catholic encyclopedia. New York: McGraw-Hill, 1967.

Cervantes de Salazar, F. México en 1554, y túmulo imperial. Mexico: Editorial Porrua, S. A., 1963.

de la Serna, J. Tratado de las idolatrías, supersticiones, dioses, ritos, hechicerías y otras costumbres gentílicas de las razas aborigenes de México. Mexico, 1953.

Foster, G. M. Culture and conquest: America's Spanish heritage. New York: Viking Fund Publications in Anthropology, No. 27, 1960.

García Mercadal, J. Viajes de extranjeros por España y Portugal. Madrid: Aguilar, 1952-1962. 3 vols.

Gatch, M. M. Death: Meaning and mortality in Christian thought and contemporary culture. New York: Seabury Press, 1969.

Green, J. S. Laughing souls: The days of the dead in Oaxaca, Mexico. San Diego: San Diego Museum of Man, 1969, Popular Series, No. 1.

Hoyos Sainz, Luis. Folkore español del culto a los muertos. Revista de Dialectologia y Tradiciones Populares, 1945, 1. (Madrid)

Huizinga, J. The waning of the Middle Ages. London: E. Arnold, 1924.

Kurtz, Leonard P. The dance of death and the macabre spirit in European literature. (Ph.D. dissertation, Columbia University, New York), 1934.

León-Portilla, M. Aztec thought and culture: A study of the ancient Nahuatl. Norman, Oklahoma: University of Oklahoma Press, 1963.

Leslie, C. M. Now we are civilized. Detroit: Wayne State University Press, 1960.

Motolinia, T. History of the Indians of New Spain. Translated and annotated by F. B. Steck. Washington, D. C.: Academy of American Franciscan History, 1951.

Parsons, E. C. Mitla, town of the souls, and other Zapotec-speaking pueblos of Oaxaca, Mexico. Chicago: University of Chicago Press, 1936.

Pfefferkorn, I. Sonora, a description of the province. Translated and annotated by T. Treutlein. Albuquerque: University of New Mexico Press, 1949.

Ruz Lhuillier, A. Costumbres funerarias de los antiguos mayas. Mexico: UNAM, 1968.

Sahagún, B. General history of the things of New Spain; Florentine codex. Translated and annotated by A. J. O. Anderson and C. E. Dibble. Santa Fe: School of American Research, 1950.

Stephens, J. L. Incidents of travel in Yucatan. New York: Harper and Brothers, 1856. 2 vols.

Thompson, J. E. S. (Ed.) Thomas Gage's travels in the New World. Norman, Oklahoma: University of Oklahoma Press, 1958.

Torquemada, J. Los veinte i un libros rituales i Monarchia Indiana. Mexico: Chaves Hayhoe, 1943.

Trapier, E. D. G. Valdés Leal, baroque concept of death and suffering in his paintings. New York: Hispanic Society of America, 1956.

Weber, F. P. Aspects of death and correlated aspects of life in art, epigram, and poetry. (4th ed. rev.) London: Lewis, 1922.

Weiser, F. X. Handbook of Christian feasts and customs. New York: Harcourt, Brace, and World, 1952.

Westheim, P. La calavera. Traducción de Mariana Frenk. Mexico: Antigua Libreria Robredo, 1953.

Whyte, F. The dance of death in Spain and Catalonia. Baltimore: Waverly Press, 1931.

CHAPTER 8

The Death Culture of Mexico and Mexican Americans[1]

Joan Moore

A CENTRAL concern with death has been recurrent in western philosophy: it has certainly not been so in western social science. As Gouldner comments, "Plato sees that death. . . is overwhelmingly and uniquely important throughout the entire life of man, which, it must be said, is still something that few social scientists as yet grasp" (1965, p. 363). The existentialists saw that it is in the knowledge of death that man defines his existence: this insight has not been picked up by cultural analysis.[2] Logically, one should be rather surprised by this neglect. Anthropological and sociological theorists have continuously sought to define human universals: whether these be functional prerequisites of social systems (à la Radcliffe-Brown and Parsons) or universal "basic questions" (à la Florence Kluckhohn), social theorists have tended to focus on how cultures relate to the natural environment, to sex, to dependent children—but rarely to death.

This is unfortunate. Death is the ultimate human weakness, the ultimate limitation, and every culture must conceptualize weakness and limitation. Gouldner's analysis of classic Greek culture, in which death was recognized but bitterly resented, illuminates both the major themes and the strains within Greek society. A similar analysis of American culture, in which death is also resented but is *not* recognized—rather is suppressed, or denied—might be extremely useful. Suppression of death in American and northern European cultures has been repeatedly discussed (see, for example, Gorer 1967; Kalish 1969). Occasionally it has been suggested that this suppression has a functional

---

[1] Partially supported by USPHS 1-RO1-MH-16537.
[2] See Choron, 1963 for the existentialists' views of death.

relationship to other elements of American culture. In particular, it is a logical concomitant of the American faith in the ability to master the environment. The conviction that the physical, social, and psychological environments *can* be controlled and manipulated to man's purposes is seriously challenged by man's failure to master his own fate.[3] The fact that every man must die is thus perhaps best managed in a culture like ours by denial. Particularly interesting is the notion that we must protect children from death. Children, who are most sensitive to learning the cultural priorities, must be shielded from the fact of human mortality. American children, who must grow up to transcend human limitations, must not be permitted even to become aware of the ultimate human limitation. The avoidance of death by social scientists is just part of the overall cultural pattern.

The contemporary American treatment of death, like the ancient Greek, appears to relate to core concerns of those two cultures, in both cases, achievement and power. The handling of death in any American minority sub-culture, therefore, must be of particular interest. American minorities have been the victims of the American emphasis on achievement; American minorities have been characterized by their powerlessness. How then, would a stigmatized, low-achieving, powerless segment of an achievement-oriented, power-oriented society face death? Would they resent it as much? Would they deny it as much? Or would one of the adaptations to their status be to recognize the pervasiveness of death and cope with it—or accept it? What would be the variations within the group? For example, would "achievers" be more—or less—likely than the middle-class Anglo to deny death? Once attitudes toward death are put into a broader context, somewhat more interesting sociological questions can be raised. And these questions, in turn, relate to psychological issues of personal adjustment to bereavement and to the individual's own death.

THE DEATH CULTURE OF MEXICO

The minority discussed in this paper—the Mexican Americans—

[3] The incompatibility between death and an achievement-oriented culture is perhaps illuminated in Greek culture by the bitter resentment of death—and also by the allied notion that "to wish for immortality is *hybris*, " (Gouldner 1965, p. 116). In contemporary terms, a doctor insightfully relates the normal medical man's avoidance of death to his sense of outrage and disillusionment at his dying patient's "betrayal" (Kasper 1959).

offers complications when we try to answer these questions. This is largely because the "home" culture—Mexico—has such an elaborate concern with death. Fifteenth century Spain had its own death culture, but with the Aztecs the Spanish encountered what Eric Wolf (1959, p. 145) calls a "fanatic obsession with blood and death." Wolf echoes the reactions of hundreds of European observers when he goes on to call the extent of human sacrifice "unique," in that "no other people on earth has felt it necessary to immolate thousands of victims annually to assure the balance of the heavens."[4] The Europeans not only observed death, but also brought death on a massive scale, with a devastating series of plagues shortly after the Conquest. It may well be that the very high death rate in the early years of Spanish occupation of Mexico facilitated the blending of Indian and Spanish death cultures. Whatever the cause, there is little doubt that contemporary Mexican rituals represent a continuity with Indian rituals: Indian food, incense, and flowers are, for example, presented to the dead on the Catholic holiday of All Saints Day (see Fergusson 1934; Green 1969). There is also little doubt that contemporary observers of Mexican life reiterate the early Spaniards' observation that death, per se, remains important in Mexican culture as a whole. For example, Serge Eisenstein focuses an important section of his Mexican films, *Day in the Sun*, on death. He moves from the funeral of a peon to a playful look at the Day of the Dead; sugar skulls become a grim commentary on the misery of the peons. A commentator on death's treatment in Western art is disturbed by contemporary Mexican depiction of death in art. She finds the work of the great revolutionary artist Posada "macabre," and chooses not to discuss his work; the preoccupation of Siqueiros and Orozco with Death symbols is noted in passing (Gottlieb 1959, p. 168). A contemporary Mexican art historian comments that Mexican art of the twentieth century has been preoccupied with two themes: revolution and death.[5] The Mexican literateur, Octavio Paz, generalizes: "We are seduced by death . . . . Our relations with death are intimate—more intimate, perhaps, than those of any other people" (1961, p. 58, 59).

[4] "Assuring the balance of the heavens" by sacrifice surely betrays an uncertainty about man's capacity to master nature.

[5] Francisco Gaona, in his lecture on Contemporary Mexican Art presented at The University of California, Riverside, February 26, 1970.

We made the statement that the "home culture" of Mexico confounds the question of how a powerless American minority would cope subculturally with death in a dominant system whose denial and resentment of death is linked with a cultural emphasis on mastery of the environment. There is considerable evidence from Mexicans themselves that the home culture of Mexico is far from sure of its capacity to master the environment. Anthropologists like Kluckhohn may see this in a positive light, as a cultural value on being in "harmony with the environment." The Mexican philosopher Ramos, like Paz, has a more depressing view: he attempts to "psychoanalyze" his culture, in Adlerian fashion. His general thesis is that the Mexican *"feels* inferior . . . . for the majority of Mexicans it constitutes a collective illusion which results from measuring man against the very high scales of values corresponding to highly developed countries" (1962, p. 57). Ramos argues that Mexicans of all class levels continuously struggle with a sense of impotence. For the lower class person, referred to by Ramos as the *pelado* (or peeled person), "his real position in life . . . is a nullity" (p. 59). The *pelado* is aware of this, and his style of life is an attempt to conceal his self-defined weakness from himself and others. "Mexican distrust" of self and others, Ramos argues, is such that "the future is a preoccupation which he has banished from his consciousness. . . . He has therefore suppressed from his life one of its most important dimensions—the future" (p. 65).

Thus the culture of Mexico may not only be characterized by an interest in death which strongly contrasts with denial and rejection in American culture, but also may be characterized by a pervasive anxiety about man's capacity to dominate and control his environment—again, in sharp contrast with the United States. Unfortunately, there is little in the social science literature on Mexico to confirm or deny the generalizations of writers like Paz and Ramos. The most significant work on the topic is the recent book by Oscar Lewis, *A Death in the Sanchez Family.* But Lewis' work, like his other books, is designed to show how one person's "life and death reflected the culture of poverty in which she lived" (1969). Thus, though Lewis' participants recount the experiences attending Guadalupe's death, wake, and burial, the underlying thread unifying the book is less on the norms and the extent to which a particular death reflects those norms, and more on the struggling, exaltations, and degradations involved in burying this woman. To be sure, the informants continually bewail the pains of being Mexican and the pains of being poor—in somewhat the fashion of a Victorian novel. However the book as a whole does not help much in the task of cultural analysis; nor does it present very much systematic evidence on the question of how heavily the culture of Mexico emphasizes individual achievement and the attainment of control over the environment. Thus the proposition that Mexican culture recognizes and is concerned with death and that this culture does not insist on mastery of the environment must remain at the level of hypothesis.

The general point made earlier stands, however. It is in fact amplified by this speculation about Mexican culture. Death will be a special issue in a deprived subsegment of a society in which denial and rejection of death in the larger system are associated with a drive toward power and mastery. It will be particularly interesting for a subsegment of a culture as different as that of Mexico. How this issue is resolved subculturally is a question for research; variation in the mode of resolution *within* the subculture is another major question. How one minority (Mexicans) compares with another (Blacks) is yet another question, when the two minorities may have a common factor in their position in the United States but may differ drastically with regard to "home culture." The remainder of this paper is addressed to a task that may be conceived as preparatory to research on such issues. It is a compilation of data and observations on death among Mexican Americans. Even this analysis must be considered preliminary, since it is based on rather scanty evidence.

NEGLECT OF DEATH IN LITERATURE ON
MEXICAN AMERICANS

There is very little in literature on Mexican Americans relating specifically to what might be termed the "death culture," either in the very poor, almost totally impotent past, or in the more recent, less desperate present. One difficulty has been that Mexican Americans have produced few visual or verbal cultural artifacts that lend themselves to analysis, with the exclusion of New Mexico, with its dying tradition of folk art. The present art and literature being produced in the Chicano movement provides an opportunity for analysis of how often and in what manner death themes are managed. An interesting and manageable research project, for example, would be a comparison of death themes in Chicano and in counterpart Black literature. But on the whole, the cultural artifacts of Mexican Americans have been remarkable in their absence. This means that the phenomenological significance of death in the Mexican American culture cannot be presented to the observer apart from the perceptual screens of his own conceptual apparatus.

One would expect that even Anglo observers would have looked at the Mexican American death culture. In a poor, Catholic, large-family group like the Mexicans, death is a crisis for both family and community. In fact, observers of earlier immigrant groups in the East noted the burial societies as among the earliest ethnic voluntary associations. In some groups they have been significant in capital accumulation. There is almost no mention in the literature of burial societies among Mexican Americans. Even superficial questioning among elderly Mexican Americans today will reveal their importance, particularly in the past. They had little impact on capital accumulation. They were not investment clubs like the Christmas clubs; rather, they were like an office pool for a girl getting married. When a Mexican member died, each member was assessed for a funeral. In substance, these old Mexican American mutualistas formalized the procedure outlined by Lewis during Guadalupe's funeral, when a collection bowl was placed near the coffin during the long wake. These groups still survive, and may still be significant in poorer areas of the Southwest as well as among today's old people.[6] There is little question that such associations would have been a major feature of communal self-help for Mexican immigrants in a hostile new society. The death of a member of a Mexican immigrant community appears

[6] In 1970, a young student at the University of California, Riverside, told me of a mutualista that his wife belonged to until she married. The group at that time consisted of about 600 members, descendants of a colony of Mexican immigrants who had settled in San Gabriel, California. There were two classes of funeral; 60 cents and $1.60. Even in 1970, that was enough to amplify family funds and provide for "a decent funeral." This student was surprised to find that "mutualistas are alive and well": he had not heard of any such groups in his own community in Los Angeles.

in fact to have been defined as a community problem, not only as a problem for the bereaved family. The burial societies, as in other immigrant groups, were apparently a collective mode of meeting what initially appeared to be an economic crisis, but which was actually a crisis in community solidarity. Certainly the burial society and its functions for contemporary aging Mexican Americans is a topic of considerable interest; one wonders why it has been neglected in past research.

The burial society is mentioned here because it has been found significant in counterpart groups studied by Anglo social scientists and is significant in a wide variety of contexts, ranging from economic to communal. One's curiosity about the neglect of death in past literature on Mexican Americans becomes even greater after even the most superficial interviewing about the topic.[7] Uniformly, one meets the flat assertion that the funeral is the single most significant family ceremony among Mexican Americans. It far outstrips marriage, baptism, or any other family or church-related rite of passage—and there are many accounts of the latter in the literature. Family members from remote points make a special effort to come together for a funeral, particularly for that of an old person. The effort is far greater than for other family ceremonies. At a recent funeral, one out-of-town relative is quoted as remarking "Why do we always have to wait for a funeral to get together: why don't we kill a goat?" While an elaborate symbolic analysis might be made of just that statement, even a superficial analysis indicates the recognized importance of funerals as occasions for family solidarity. One begins to conceive of the neglect of death in the study of Mexican Americans as yet another indicator of the American cultural denial and rejection of death, especially in recent decades.

In addition to the importance of death and funerary behavior to an understanding of family and communial bonds, there is another strong reason for the study of death. Patterns of behavior about death and bereavement are among areas that are most conservative and most resistant to change of any culture or subculture. For this reason, its study should have high priority among

[7] I am indebted to Lorenzo Campbell and Benjamin Gonzales, in particular, for their observations, on which I have drawn heavily in this paper. In addition, David Leon, Norma Leon, and Jose Tapia offered valuable insights.

social scientists interested in persistence and change in ethnic subcultures in this country.

The conservatism of funerary behavior can be illustrated in Mexico itself. Indian customs were incorporated into the Spanish Catholic rites—both on the Day of the Dead and at the normal funeral. Candles, water, flowers, food, and incense are provided for the dead in the villages on the Day of the Dead. The particular artifacts demonstrate continuity with ancient times. These observances survive in the order listed as people move to the cities. For example, Lewis describes Guadalupe's celebrations on the Day of the Dead as including candles, water, and flowers; food and incense had disappeared. Why should these survive? Partly because of the intensity of emotions aroused by even such an apparently remote gesture as the visit to the cemetery on the Day of the Dead. Though most published accounts of those celebrations in Mexico emphasize the quiet cheerfulness of the occasion, one of my Mexican-born colleagues has a very different memory. He left Mexico when he was a child, and one of his most intense memories is of the terror inspired by the ceremonies on the Day of the Dead. The Day meant a terrifying visit with his mother to feed his ancestors—he remembers them as mummified, ancient, and awe-inspiring. These ancestors were *not* those of the "normal American"—grandparents or great-grandparents—but remote in time. They had been there for centuries, according to him. This is another reason for the conservatism of this area of life—particularly in "the old country." We in this nation have only a few generations behind us at the most; to the Mexican a visit to the graveyard is potentially a visit to his personal antiquity and his connection with the land. To a Mexican American, the cultural artifacts of death in Mexico may have a very special place in his memories of his homeland, profoundly affecting his view of death in this society. Full knowledge of the "homeland" death culture does not give more than a remote knowledge of what that effect may be; he was not fully socialized in the culture of Mexico, and his partial socialization may have, as in this case, intensified certain aspects of the death culture in his memory.

Another important reason for the conservatism of customs connected with death is that it is generally the old people who die, and conscious efforts are made by their surviving young relatives to "do what they would have wanted." Among the young Mexican Americans I talked with, funeral ceremonies given for grand-parents often violated the belief of the survivors. For example, one old man with a Protestant wife and non-practicing children was given a conservative Catholic burial. In another family, the atheistic sons of an old man not only buried him in the most conservative Mexican church in Los Angeles, but his male rela-tives went fully through the ritual—against their own principles. There is thus a strong element of truth in the Catholic clerical cliché that "they always come back to the Church to die." How-ever, far from being a reconversion of the straying Catholic, I believe that this "return to the Church" is part of the complex of general cultural retentiveness around death and bereavement.

THE DEATH OF AN OLD MAN:
THE MEXICAN AMERICAN NORM

What follows here is the result of a preliminary exploration into the "normal funeral" in a Mexican American family of a metropolitan area. In a very real sense, this is a description of norms: what *ought* to happen with the death of a person who *ought* to die—an old person. Following this, the discussion will turn to departures from these norms. The departures may be of several types: the wrong kind of person may die—a young person— or the death may occur in the wrong kind of setting—accidentally, for example. From this, we may raise questions about variations on the norms—the effect of mobility, intermarriage, and so on.

As far as I can gather, the crisis periods—the death, wake, funeral mass, and burial—are essentially more emotional and more participant variants of the standard American Catholic ritual. (By "more participant" I simply mean that everybody participates publicly.) Or, to put it the other way around, they are sterilized and tidied-up versions of what Lewis describes in his book on Guadalupe's death. After the death and its certification, the body is moved to the funeral home. This, an intrusion of state law into family customs, removes the most emotional scenes into the im-personal setting of the funeral home. In most Anglo funerals the immediate family is not visible; in the Mexican American funeral they sit in front. In most Anglo funerals children do not partici-pate; apparently this is not the case in Mexican American funerals. There is greater participation by all ages and degrees of involvement with the dead person than in the normal American funeral.

The rosary is said in Spanish and sets the tone for the rest of the ceremony. In Los Angeles, it is only the old people who know the Spanish rosary, and it is the old people, particularly the old women, who come into their own during the funeral and the succeeding events. The old women wail. According to one young informant, they sound much like the little old ladies in Mexican churches who wail during their private devotions. A young man from New Mexico states that in the rural areas of that state there are still professional wailers—lloronas—and apparently the possibility of such a practice is not altogether remote even in Los Angeles. One young Angeleno said that his grandfather's funeral was invaded by a total stranger wailing; it was assumed that she would want money.

After the rosary we progress to the viewing—and touching, and kissing—of the body. At least the older people touch; the younger informants protested this action. Condolences are then shifted from the dead person to his family and the wake moves to the home, for talking, eating and drinking. During this period it appears that the most immediately bereaved persons are the targets of the strongest reintegrative efforts: old friends talk endlessly about old times, though not necessarily about the dead person.

The funeral mass the next day begins to shift the focus to the whole family and community. Segregation by sex continues, with the men often on the porch of the church, women inside. On the porch a frequent topic of the conversation may be the meaning of the dead person to the family's position in the community. Pallbearers reflect this communal linkage—not only sons and grandsons, but fellow members of the Knights of Columbus or of the G. I. Forum or other civic associations are involved. Family reintegration also continues to be important in the postburial activities.

The days and weeks after the burial are in some respects the most interesting. An Anglo might expect that the deceased would have been adequately honored by traditional funeral and burial and that the family would then "modernize" and do nothing.

This was not the case among the people I talked with. Novenas, grave visits, and so on, punctuate the family's life for several months after the death. One young anti-religious boy got up with his mother and sister every Sunday at 5 A.M. for early mass, a visit to his aunt's grave, and back to church again. He made no protest, and felt full respect.

It is during this post-burial period that the controls of the older over the younger generation are reasserted. As previously mentioned, children are active participants in all events. They are expected to be affected. For a period after the burial the family lives quietly; social activities are sharply reduced. In some families, radio and television are turned off. Girls are kept from dating. (One young woman was devastated because her grandfather died the day of her senior prom.) Though dates are also proscribed for boys, they manage to evade some of the more stringent controls—as they do, and are expected to do, with other areas alike. In general, however, for several months after the death of an old person, family controls are reasserted over all members. Demand for observance of the controls is made in the name of respect. There is no reference at all to a religious rational, e.g., that behavior after the funeral could affect the fate of the dead soul. In general, the value placed on respect in the Mexican American culture has probably been greatly underestimated as a conservative force. Respect for elders, for tradition, for authority, for religion, has been the basis of appeals by parents with school-aged children, by politicians attempting to control militancy, by even such a militant as Ceasar Chavez in his union's relations with the Catholic church. It is in the name of "respect" that Mexican American men temporarily relinquish their anti-religious behavior. "Respect" thus involves a test of maturity and a behavioral statement about priority of values. One "abandons" principle in favor of alleviating the discomfort of other human beings—most importantly, of one's grieving female relatives—and one does so in the name of traditional respect.

There are, of course, many features of this account common to other Americans, particularly to Catholics of southern European descent. But there are some that are distinctive. Family reintegration at the funeral depends on the sacrifices made by the large-family to be present at the ceremony. The family spends money it can ill afford in order to get a child or grandchild home. It notifies cousins who have been invisible for years: the entire family must rally. Of course, for this to occur one must have a large family. Familism is reaffirmed at the funeral of an old head or spouse of one of the subfamilies. Though not specifically "Mexican," familism of this sort is characteristically "Mexican."

Just as the family must rally, so must the community rally. This means both the community of the past (brought in for some through the mechanism of the mutualista) and the present day community. The family's link to the past—its historical status in the community—is reaffirmed. Its linkage in the present–day is re-established. In this fashion, the funeral helps maintain ethnic cohesiveness. Rallying of family and community revives the sense of historical identity, which is the core of ethnic identity. Men and women who are otherwise assimilated, who live and work with Anglos, "return," at least temporarily, for the funeral.

REQUISITES OF THE "NORMAL" FUNERAL

Wake, funeral mass, burial, and mourning for the old man thus may function to revive both family and ethnic feelings. In this sense, the funeral is "Mexican," no matter what may be shared with other Catholic ceremonies. However, this normal ceremony, even for the old person, has some important requisites, and it is with the consideration of such requisites that we begin to approach the topic of variations upon the normative theme.

The normal ceremony as described requires a large family with a "normal" age–sex distribution, in a reasonably meaningful relationship to a community of the past or the present. Today, for many old people in Los Angeles, much of the meaningful relationship to the community of the past depends on the shared problems of the immigrant generation. The work groups of the 1920s and 1930s, the mutualistas, are aspects of life for the generation born around the turn of the century and migrating from Mexico to the United States. Many Mexican Americans, even in Los Angeles, did not have the experience of immigration, and the "community of the past" for most Mexican Americans in New Mexico, with its predominantly "charter-member" contingence, would be entirely different. So also would the community of the past in Texas, where the generational experiences have been quite different from those in California.

Community solidarity may be a requisite for attaining the kinds of reintegrative functions, on the personal and family level, that have been discussed here. But the bases for community solidarity—both present and past—may differ widely from one area to another of the Southwest, or even within Los Angeles. Sampling for community values is a difficult problem in the study of Mexican Americans.

Another requisite for a normal funeral is the capacity to muster enough money to bury the person decently. The meaning of "enough money" or of "decent burial" is an interesting topic of research. Clearly, a certain level of expense and a certain number of people are necessary for a socially effective funerary drama. There must also be permissible variations in the scale of expense for people of varying means, but at any given level of expectations, it would appear that the funeral expenses represent a financial strain. (In fact, it may be that financial strain is part of the expectations.) The funeral costs entail not only the direct costs of coffin, burial plot, funeral home, and mass, but also expenditures in assembling the family from distant points, housing and feeding family and guests, and so on.

There is an important research question involved in the matter of expenditures. Raising money is the most essential of the behind-the-scene actions that may be lumped together as the non-ceremonial aspects of behavior around death. What are the norms about family member's contributions? Who should bear the major burden? Are loan companies involved? If so, who manages the financial negotiations? In Oscar Lewis' study of a funeral in Mexico City, money is a paramount theme: there is no surviving spouse, and the male relatives are too indigent to take complete charge. The negative feelings between survivors in Guadalupe's family were exacerbated by the financial problems of the burial. In such destitute families, which also exist among Mexican Americans, is there still an attempt to meet some "normal" funeral ideal? Or is the funeral ceremony attenuated and shrunken? Do mutualistas survive in such poverty-level families as a way of meeting the financial crisis?

In addition to family, community, and money as necessary conditions for a "good funeral," there is one final point to be mentioned. That is, people have to be prepared to play their roles in the funeral and its aftermath. "Preparation" may mean several things. First, of course, there is socialization to the funeral roles. Mexican American children attend funerals frequently, as a rule, and they learn the behavior appropriate to men and women of different ages and relationships to the deceased. In a brief pilot study, young Mexican American children were asked to tell a story about a picture of an old dead woman laid out with no coffin: responses were entirely on the factual level: "that must be Mexico"; "they must be very poor if they can't afford a coffin"; and so on—suggesting a relatively easy familiarity with the facts of death.[8] Thus, not only is funerary role behavior subject to socialization, but so also is the general capacity to deal with human death and funerals on the cognitive level. This general capacity may in the past (and for today's middle-aged Mexican American) have been related to the rural background from which this population is largely derived. Experience with animal death on the farm may have been frequent and have served some kind of preparatory function denied to children who were as products of urban socialization.

We may speculate about a more subtle kind of "preparation" as well. The accounts of a normal funeral note the prominence of women. Unlike the secular socially-oriented party, women rather than men are the focus of interest and emotion. To be sure, there are similarities between the normative role of women in funerals and their traditional roles elsewhere. They are segregated, they are expected to be emotional. But women's prominence in the funeral suggests that they are in some way especially "prepared" for this role, that death may be in some way a special confirmation of some aspect of their normal role. This revives the question discussed at the outset of this paper—namely, the question of the recognition and concern with death in the Mexican American subculture. In this context, there was a suggestive theme recurrent in interviews with young men, all of whom remembered aunts and grandmothers shaking their forefingers and warning, "you'll be sorry when I'm dead!" Although the words are hackneyed, it is rather unlikely that most Anglo children have actually heard

[8] I am indebted to Jennifer Hurstfield for this observation.

them from women of the older generation. More often, in the larger culture, it is children who warn their parents. It is, of course, dangerous to generalize from a few anecdotes, but it is generally acknowledged that suppression of women is not unknown among Mexican Americans. Could it not be that women's "preparation" for prominence during the funeral is related to their suppression in everyday life? Certainly such an interpretation would be consonant with the macro-cultural interpretation initally made in this paper. If funerary roles are related to everyday suppression, this is a topic well worth investigating in any study of adjustments to death and bereavement.

VARIATIONS ON THE NORMATIVE PATTERN

When any of the requisites for the "normal" funeral are lacking (those suggested here, or others), presumably the funeral and its aftermath are variant, or perhaps even deviant, in failing to fulfill the functions suggested. However, there are variations within the "norm," i.e., there are circumstances under which the ceremonial and nonceremonial aspects of death can serve reintegrative functions on personal, familial and communal levels, but which are quite different from those described as "normal."

As an illustration, the death of an old woman is normatively quite different from that of an old man. To the extent that the family structure represented traditional roles, the old woman is more likely to have played a more supportive, more sympathetic role vis-á-vis survivors than is the old man. The death of an old woman is more likely than that of an old man to evoke more straightforward grief. Old men are likely to evoke ambivalence. They may have been family founders, and in their old age no longer possessed of much power to cause pain. But given the facts of life for most Mexicans in the 1920s, '30s and '40s, many if not most old men are likely to have been poor economic providers, often to have generated family problems during the search for work. Moreover, most were probably relatively impotent in their dealings with American institutions, and hence provided weak role models for their sons and grandsons. In short, there were many marital and parental problems around the behavior of men in traditional Mexican American families of the past generation, and the death of an old man is different for all concerned than the death of an old woman.

Another illustration of a variant pattern may be seen in the generational problem raised earlier in the discussion of requisites for communal solidarity. While most of today's old dying Mexican Americans in Los Angeles represent a specifiable generational experience, many do not. Some may have immigrated from Mexico just a few years ago, following their recently immigrated children. Some may be fifth or sixth generation Angelenos. Los Angeles presents some real challenges to the student of Mexican Americans. As a magnet for immigration from the entire Southwest and Mexico, the dying old people are very likely to have come from a wide range of places, and to have been in Los Angeles a widely varying length of time. The nature of observances around the funeral and after, and the degree to which community and ethnic solidarity can be reasserted, is obviously related to the family's history in the area. Also, many subtleties in the observances vary with the cultural "distance" from Mexico. Variations can thus be expected in Los Angeles itself with respect to these matters.

A final point may be made concerning variations around the norm. The funeral described as normal is a Catholic funeral. Clearly there will be variations within Catholicism: for example, not all old people are buried from the conservative sanctuario of Guadalupe. Religiosity—or intensity of practice—within the family is another basis of variation: in the post-funeral period, novenas are an important vehicle by which family authority and family solidarity are reasserted. Obviously, the degree of religiosity in the family will affect the extent to which such traditional modes of behavior can be comfortably utilized. Finally, some 10 percent of the Mexican American population is not Catholic at all, but Protestant.

DEPARTURES FROM THE NORM

Whether the death of an upwardly mobile or relatively assimilated man or woman represents a departure from the Mexican American norm or a variation on it is a question involving values. Statistically, it may not in itself be a very important question, at least for today's oldsters, because so few have achieved occupational mobility or any degree of assimilation. There are questions related to both social class and ethnic mobility in the middle-aged generation, however, that are relevant. What, for example, is the upwardly mobile man to do about his father's death? Following the model of Yankee City, described by Lloyd Warner (1959), he may well use his father's funeral to establish his own status symbolically—perhaps a burial at Forest Lawn rather than at Calvary Cemetery, perhaps an "Anglo" service rather than a Mexican one. Superficially such status-oriented burials might be seen as a special symbol of "respect" for the dead—an especially "decent" burial. On the other hand, they might well be seen as betrayals of family and ethnic custom, and sources of conflict among the survivors. Status mobility and death are profoundly important issues, as Warner has shown, and well worth a special investigation, even in a relatively non-mobile population such as the Mexican Americans.

On the other extreme, we must raise the question of poverty again, in the context of deviance. The only person interviewed from a "multi-problem" slum family remembered funerals as times of family tension and fights—not as times of family integration. Mutual accusations of neglect of the deceased, other charges and countercharges, guilt and hostility, were not resolved during the funerary observances. Obviously this is not a problem of lack of money alone, but perhaps, of the accumulated tensions that attend slum living. One of the norms during the funeral and its aftermath is that conflict is suppressed. If poverty life and, perhaps, other sources of family tension can produce a violation of that extremely strong norm, how are such tensions and conflicts resolved or, alternatively, acted out?

Obviously, both poverty and mobility may affect the capacity of the family to reassert its integration—both internally and with the ethnic community—thus impairing the functions of the funeral and its aftermath. So also may other sources of family divisivness, such as migration, mixed marriage, and so on.

The final question relating to deviant patterns are those which occur when the "wrong" person dies, or dies in the "wrong" way or in the "wrong" place. Most cultures have some tradition about the special fate of the "wrong" people. Pregnant women have a special malice toward women who died in childbirth; men who die in battle have a special niche; children, especially infants, go to a special fate after death. Both standard Christian mythology and archaic Mexican mythology provide special fates for such "wrong" people. And, in a poor population—in all minority populations in the United States—such wrong people die more frequently than in the larger population.

Little more will be done here than raise this question. Only one point will be pursued: the death of a man killed in Vietnam. Such deaths have a very special meaning in a minority population. In pro-war areas or families, commonly in south Texas, for example, the high death rate among chicanos is taken as evidence of the collective virtues of the Mexican American people—their machismo, their willingness to sacrifice for their country, and so on. Community definition of such a death will affect the way in which the bereaved family becomes reintegrated in the community. In a macabre sense, a dead soldier can become a piece of family "capital," a contribution to the enhancement of the family's standing in the community. Alternatively, in a community with a different definition of the war and which defined the high chicano death rate as genocide, a funeral of a Vietnam casualty can become an occasion for violent alienation from the larger society.

In the cases of the Vietnam or other "wrong" person's death, there is no problem with the person himself, just with his status at the manner of his death. A very serious question arises in the case of a death which occurs in pursuit of some illegal action. Thirty-nine Mexican Americans in Los Angeles County died in 1969 of narcotics overdoses; an unknown, though small, number died in prison or were killed by police. Though this is statistically negligible, and though it is probably not researchable, speculation about such deaths might be fruitful. The family must cope with a member labelled as a wrongdoer. What factors would be associated with, for example, the family's decision to conceal or, alternatively, to confront that legal label? An ostensible suicide in a sheriff's lockup may reintegrate the family and the community by uniting them against officialdom, for example, as apparently occurred recently. In several instances, deaths at the hands of police have become occasions for community organization and, thus, for ethnic militancy. This is a very meaningful departure from the normal pattern of reintegration of family and community. Suicides and homicides represent another version of this problem of "deviant deaths."

A final point may be made with regard to the death of a "normal," i.e., old, person in an abnormal place. Death in the county hospital may be a matter for deep family bitterness. One young man remembers the death of his beloved grandmother with great anger. Children under sixteen were not allowed to visit her. He was the only one of some ten grandchildren old enough to go. This was a deep violation of emotional and family norms, with an ensuing resentment against the bureaucratic norms. Minority group members often mount guard over hospitalized relatives to ensure their adequate care and to keep them company. In the case of this young man, moving the family in for a twenty-four hour watch during her dying days meant a prolonged battle with the institution. Few Mexican American families would have the emotional resources or the persistence to accomplish such a victory, though it is highly probable that many share this family's sense of outrage that their loved member was left by the agency to die inhumanely. Nursing and convalescent home deaths may entail similar violations of normal expectations for managing both death and funeral. In these two illustrations the institutional quality of the place of death has been emphasized; death by street accident, for example, probably has little special meaning because there is no organized influence countering the operation of family norms.

GENERAL COMMENTS

Deviant, variant, or normal death and funerary practice all raise questions about how the reintegrative functions operate among Mexican Americans. The point has been made that the "normal" funeral of an old man and its aftermath reintegrates the family and its special history with community and ultimately with ethnic history. However, the consideration of variant and especially of deviant funerals raises another aspect of this question: will such integration be hostile to the larger society? Will the reaffirmation of past ethnic identity generate pride—or yet more ambivalence about the past of the group? Research into the funeral customs must not blind the researcher to the fact that this is a minority in this society—a relatively powerless segment, whose powerlessness is nowhere more evident than in its troubles and private ceremonies.

The point was also made that the normal funeral and later

observances reinforce general norms. This raises an important methodological issue: in the interviews conducted for this paper there was almost total consensus on the norms. The individual, private, feelings of discomfort, or of disapproval for the practices, e.g., religious practices, were overwhelmed into insignificance. Thus one might conclude that the function of the funeral is *general* norm reinforcement which operates by resolving the discrepancy between the individual's feelings and the group norm. This resolution is accomplished by both the highly charged emotional atmosphere and by the prevailing altruism, in which "principles" take second place to comforting the most grief-stricken relatives. But this, of course, is *not* resolution, and the norms that are being reinforced are of the most general kind—humanitarian, for example, rather than specifically ethnic. Religion is not strengthened, but family bonds are, if things go well, reinforced. Perhaps most important, human needs are openly expressed, acknowledged, and met.

Death is the ultimate human limitation. Subcultural as well as individual adaptations to this limit on human potential reflect group status as well as group tradition. They reflect group and individual strengths, accomplishments, failures, and needs, as they are expressed and managed through a rapidly changing and increasingly heterogeneous tradition.

REFERENCES

Choron, J. 1963. *Death and western thought.* New York: Collier Books.

Fergusson, Erna. 1934. *Fiesta in Mexico.* New York: Knopf.

Gorer, G. 1967. *Death, grief and mourning.* New York: Anchor Books.

Gottlieb, Carla, 1959. Modern art and death. In *The meaning of death,* ed. H. Feifel, pp. 158–88. New York: McGraw Hill.

Gouldner, A. W. 1965. *Enter Plato.* New York: Basic Books.

Green, Judith S. 1969. *Laughing souls.* San Diego: Museum of Man Popular Series No. 1.

Kalish, R. A. 1969. The effects of death upon the family. In *Death and dying,* ed. L. Pearson, pp. 79–107. Cleveland: Case Western Reserve Univ. Press.

Kasper, A. M. 1959. The doctor and death. In *The meaning of death,* ed. H. Feifel, pp. 259–70. New York: McGraw Hill.

Lewis, O. 1969. *A death in the Sanchez family.* New York: Random House.

Paz, O. 1961. *The labyrinth of solitude.* New York: Grove Press.

Ramos, S. 1962. *Profile of man and culture in Mexico.* Austin: Univ. Tex. Press.

Warner, W. L. 1959. *The living and the dead.* New Haven: Yale Univ. Press.

Wolf, E. 1959. *Sons of the shaking earth.* Chicago: Univ. Chicago Press.

CHAPTER 9

The Black Experience
with Death: A Brief Analysis
through Black Writings

Maurice Jackson

All people die, but not all people die alike. It is a truism to say that people from all groups die, but the immense influence of group membership upon the experience with death is far less obvious, as Durkheim argued so cogently, in the case of suicide (Durkheim, 1950). Nowhere does this fact seem more evident than in contrasting the black experience with death in America with the experience of other ethnic groups. Documentation of these differences is not found in the literature of the behavioral or psychiatric sciences (Vernon, 1970). For example, there is no systematic attention given to black mortality in a recent volume (Kiser, 1970) treating the demographic aspects of the black community, although Dr. Irene B. Taeuber, one of the participants, said that mortality statistics is the best measure of the relative status of blacks and whites in America. Therefore we need to turn to historical accounts and folk arts for the most vivid expression of this intense experience. In so doing, the black experience with death and those features which seem to highlight the black experience are stressed.

Statistics do exist in abundance; but they do not tell all the story. The number, percentage, rate, incidence, and prevalence, who died from what illness, at what age, with what lack of medical care are carefully documented. We need to turn to history for a fuller sense of the black experience with death and the interpretation of that experience.

Davidson (1961) estimates that between 15 and 50 million Africans were taken from their native lands in chains and deposited, often in the same chains, on the coast of the Western Hemisphere. Most likely even greater numbers never finished the trip (Tannebaum, 1963). Perhaps as many as 100 million and certainly over 30 million African blacks were forcibly recruited to begin the journey. Those who failed to survive were victims of starvation, suffocation, drowning, suicide, disease, and the whippings, beatings, mutilation, and direct killing by those who held them in bondage. Some of the deaths had strange bases, indeed. Mannix and Cowley (1970, p. 27) add to the list of causes of death, "fixed melancholy," a loss of will of slaves to live even when they were well fed, treated with kindness, and kept under relatively sanitary conditions. These conditions of death continued throughout the era of slavery. Weld (1969) presents example after example of slaves being whipped, burned, and mutilated. One female slave was whipped to death and "delivered of a dead child" while undergoing the punishment (p. 46). Another example was that of "seven poor unfortunate slaves—some chained to the floor, others with chains around their necks, fastened to the ceiling; and one poor old man, upwards of sixty years of age, chained hand and foot, and made fast to the floor in a kneeling position. His head bore the appearance of having been beaten until it was broken . . . . A woman had her back literally cooked . . . with the lash; the very bones might be seen projected through the skin!" (p. 91). Frederick Douglass described the death of his mother in most poignant terms: "I was not allowed to visit her during any part of her long illness . . . . The heartless and ghastly form of slavery rises between mother and child, even at the bed of death" (p. 54).

A further type of evidence of the unusual character of death among black people can be drawn from the laws regarding capital punishment and the form of the capital punishment itself. In nineteenth-century Virginia, for seventy-one crimes for which slaves received capital punishment, whites received only imprisonment; similarly, in Mississippi, slaves could be given a death sentence for thirty crimes for which whites would receive only a fine or imprisonment (Weld, 1969). Between 1930 and 1968, 3859 prisoners were executed under state and federal court rulings; 2066 (54 percent) of these were black (Nabrit, 1969). Other executions, such as lynchings, must also be added. According to *The Negro Almanac*, at least 3400 blacks were lynched between 1882 and 1962 (Polski and Brown, 1967).

Black death rates also exceed those of the general population in war and from disease. The rate of mortality for black soldiers in the Civil War was 40 percent higher than that for whites (Franklin, 1966); similar statistics have emerged from the Vietnamese war (Harris, 1969). Death rates for non-whites (probably 90 percent black) are higher than death rates for whites at virtually all ages (Vernon, 1970); when compared with death rates of thirteen European countries, nonwhite Americans, both male and female, young, middle-aged, and elderly, all had by a substantial percentage, the highest death rates (Metropolitan Life Statistical Bulletin, February, 1971).

SACRED AND SECULAR NORMS

The purpose of this account is not to add another horror story to the academic literature. It is, rather, to delineate a few of the more dramatic reasons for the meaning that death may have for blacks. With this as background, the foreground of the ways in which death is handled by black people will be explored.

There are at least two alternatives. First is that set of expectations which can be described as the sacred norm. This norm specifies that black people should attend to the supernatural and metaphysical concerns surrounding and following death, while de-emphasizing things of this world. Death in this context would provide an escape from this world. The sacred norm assumes that black people cannot deal effectively with death as a phenomenon in this world and, therefore, should look to and glorify another world, an afterworld.

A different set of expectations form the secular norm, which specifies that black people should view death as part of the normal life process, as an inevitable event in a naturalistic context, occurring in the world of experience. Death should be accepted as a frequent companion, and black people would not need to de-emphasize it by focussing upon a supernatural world. The secular norm assumes that death should be interpreted as natural, in spite of its obvious highly disturbing social and emotional impact.

The sacred-secular norm distinction somewhat parallels Vernon's temporal (this-world) and spiritual (other-world) interpretations of death (Vernon, 1970). However, these orientations can better be seen as obligatory, hence normative. The terms "sacred" and "secular" also carry Durkheim's meaning of "things put aside" and "things not put aside" respectively (Durkheim, 1926). The question, then, is do black people feel obliged to treat death as a thing put aside from this world (the sacred norm) or as something very much a part of this world (the secular norm)?

The usual interpretation of the behavior and rituals with which blacks approach death is that they represent virtually the epitome of the sacred approach. It will be shown why this is not the case, that indeed the very opposite is true, and that lack of historical and sociological understanding has severely limited the ability to interpret the significance of this behavior and these rituals. Even in Africa, belief in the power of the ancestral dead to affect the lives of their descendents was widespread (Herskovits, 1958). Although many contemporary behavioral scientists might consider this to be a superstition, the intent is not to debate the truth of the beliefs, but to use the example to indicate the kind of naturalistic continuity that existed between those on earth and those who had died.

SPIRITUALS AND POETRY

Since academic reports are lacking, the literature of the black people will be considered, beginning with spirituals and developing though more contemporary writings. The spirituals themselves are probably the form of black literature most open to varied interpretation. Rather than symbolizing the other-worldly phenomena that emerges from a literal translation, they should be considered as a covert form of desire for freedom, with death simultaneously representing actual death and freedom—with the obvious realization that the only freedom most of the slaves would find was to occur with death. In that light, consider the words of "Swing low, sweet chariot," with the dual symbolism of death and freedom, although sung in the context of traditional Christianity. It is not difficult to realize the consequences, had the slaves expressed their desire for freedom from slavery in more overt fashion.

Thus Brown (1958, p. 279-289) concludes that references to troubles on earth are far more numerous in Negro spirituals than are references to freedom in a Christian form of heaven. He goes further: "It is only a half-truth to see the spirituals as other-worldly. 'You take dis worl', and give me Jesus' is certainly one of the least of the refrains. In the spirituals the slave took a clear-eyed look at this world, and he revealed in tragic poetry what he saw."

Fisher is in agreement (1969). He states that "Negroes did not sing other-worldly songs like white people" (p. 182). While plantation missionaries stressed other-worldliness, not one spiritual "reflected interest in anything other than a full life here and now" (Fisher, 1969, p. 137). Even the frequent references to heaven could readily be interpreted as symbolizing a place on earth away from slavery: "Negro slaves ordinarily believed that Africa was heaven," (Fisher, 1969, p. 146), and that heaven within the United States was in the North.

Familiarity with death emphasized in the spirituals, expresses the secular norm of death with which the blacks were so familiar. First as Fisher (1969) states, the blacks were prepared to accept death. Second, familiarity with death is shown in the interpretation of death as another life on earth (Fisher, 1969). Here death provides a continuity with life. As a matter of fact until the first half of the nineteenth century,

THE BLACK EXPERIENCE WITH DEATH / 95

black people preferred to believe in African reincarnation than in Christian immortality. The popularity of the famous spiritual based upon the death and rising of Lazarus gives support for this view.

In many spirituals, neither a secular nor a sacred view of death was evident. Nonetheless, the themes of death as freedom, rest, departure, and finding peace were all very common. "Resting in the arms of Jesus" produces the image of a warm human relationship, not a mystical fantasy.

Poetry written by black authors complements this discussion of the meaning of death found in the spirituals. Paul Lawrence Dunbar (1899) continues the theme of intimate familiarity with death, an expression of the secular norm, in his poem *A Death Song*. In the poem he draws a picture of familiar physical surroundings in describing a death scene. The poem also specifies certain favorite conditions under which death is acceptable: "If I's layin' 'mong de t'ings I's allus knowed." Finally, the poem contains a definition of death as rest and release, a secular theme.

A Death Song

Lay me down beneaf de willer in de grass,
What de branch'll go a-singin' as it pass.
An' w'en I's a-layin' low,
I kin hyeah it as it go
Singin', "Sleep, my honey, tek yo' re' at las'."
Lay me nigh to whah hit meks a little pool,
An 'de watah stan's so quiet lak an' cool,
Whah de little birds in spring,
Ust to come an' drink an' sing,
An 'de chillen waded on dey way to school

Let me settle w'en my shouldahs draps dey load
Nigh enough to hyeah'de noises in 'de road;
Fu' I t'ink de las' long res',
Gwine to soothe my sperrit bes'
If I's layin' 'mong 'de t'ings I's allus knowed.

Claude McKay, in his famous poem *If We Must Die*, written in 1919, offers another definition of death which highlights the secular norm. He relates death to social relationships in this world. Death can be noble—or it can be ignoble, a death for hogs. The preferred type of death for black people is a noble death, even though it means that blacks, outnumbered and outpowered, die in fighting back.

Around the same time, James Weldon Johnson illustrated the secular norm of death by defining death, as did Dunbar, as a time of rest. In his *Go Down Death*, he says that "She is not dead," but that she has found rest through closeness with Jesus. Later in the same poem, Johnson writes of death as a reward for laboring "long in my vineyard."

A more recent poem *When I Am Dead* by Owen Dodson (1970, p. 285) explores the familiarity theme of the secular norm through underscoring familiar physical surroundings.

When I Am Dead

Now would I tread my darkness down
And wish for clover overhead;
The roots below will twine a crown
When I am dead.
The seal of color stamps too deep
For wounded flesh to live and win;
The earth is shielding and will keep
My darkness close within.[1]

CONTEMPORARY BLACK LITERATURE

The emphasis upon the secular norm of death is also found in contemporary literature written by black people. For example, Claude Brown (1965, p. 48-49) in *Manchild in the Promised Land* pointed to another definition of death as a reward, specifically for masculinity. Funerals in Harlem vary, depending upon the "toughness" of the individual involved. Among other things, funerals are ways to reward blacks who stand up to other people, especially white people. Claude stated:

> The best (church) songs were sung at the funerals for the 'bad niggers'. I learned that a bad nigger who didn't take shit from nobody' and that even the 'crackers' didn't mess with him . . . .
> One day I went to a funeral for a bad nigger. A lot of people were there, and most of them had heard about him but were seeing him for the first time. I guess they were scared to see him while he was still alive and still bad. . . . At his funeral, a lot of ladies cried, and the preacher talked about him real loud for a long time. Before the preacher started talking, somebody sang 'Before this Time Another Year' and 'Got On My Traveling Shoes.' When the preacher finished talking about him, they took the casket outside and put it down in the ground. I have seen people do that before, but I didn't think they would do it this time. It just didn't seem like the right way to treat a bad nigger, unless being dead made him not so bad any more. . . .
> Somebody would sing real good at Grandpa's funeral, and a lot of people would be there. It would have to be a big funeral, because Grandpa was a real bad and evil nigger when he was a young man.

A final example of the black norm of death as a commentary on social relationships is found in Redding's (1951, pp. 13-15) description of the death of a white person. In it Redding shows how his own life as a black person affected his view of death. Here, the death of a white person seen as symbolic of antagonistic white people, was defined as partially satisfying.

On looking out of the window of the college building at something which moved in the yard below, Redding reports:

> There would have been no shock in seeing a woman of the neighborhood dressed only in a ragged slip, but a powdery snow had fallen the night before and the day was bitter cold. When I saw the woman, who seemed quite young, she was lurching and staggering in the rear of the yard. A dog must have followed her out of the house, for one stood by the open door watching and flicking its tail dubiously. The woman's face was stiff and

---

[1] "When I am Dead" is reprinted from the volume *Powerful Long Ladder* by permission of the publisher, Farrar, Straus and Giroux, Inc. Copyright 1946 by Owen Dodson.

> vacant, but in her efforts to walk her body and limbs jerked convulsively in progressive tremors. I could not tell whether she was drunk or sick as she floundered in the snow in the yard. Pity rose in me, but at the same time something else also—a gloating satisfaction that she was white. Sharply and concurrently felt, the two emotions were of equal strength, in perfect balance, and the corporeal I fixed in a trance at the window, oscillated between them.
>
> When she was within a few steps of the outhouse, the poor woman lurched violently and pitched face downward in the snow. Somehow utterly unable to move, I watched her convulsive struggles for several minutes. The dog came down the yard meanwhile, whining piteously, and walked stiff-legged around the white and almost naked body. The woman made a mess in the snow and then lay still.
>
> Finally I turned irresolutely and went into the corridor. There was the entrance door and near it the telephone. I could have gone out and a few steps would have brought me to the yard where the woman lay and I could have tried to rouse someone or myself taken her into the house, I went to the telephone and called the police.[2]

He read in the newspaper the next morning that a twenty-six year old woman had died of exposure followed an epileptic seizure, suffered while alone.

Redding concluded that his experience as a Negro in America had fostered his reaction to a dying white person. In his words, "The experience of my Negroness, in a section where such experiences have their utmost meaning in fear and degradation, cancelled out humaneness."

A WORLDLY VIEW OF DEATH

The magnitude and quality of the experience that black people have with death, has been documented. It has been shown that the norm governing that experience may best be described as secular rather than sacred. In short, it appears that the magnitude and quality of death among black people have resulted in a practical, worldly view of death. Practicality may then represent a value orientation among black people that permeates other activities. Therefore, efforts to explain the behavior of black people in other-worldly terms have to be re-examined and eventually discarded if this study is supported by future findings and analysis. The results also have implications for other activities e. g., "immediate gratification." The findings suggest that "immediate gratification," to the extent it exists, reflects a practical interpretation of the use of resources and not an impractical world view.

This evaluation must be viewed as explorative rather than definitive. Its results point to the need for scientifically planned and executed studies of the character of death among black people. Many important questions need to be answered. What are the similarities and dissimilarities in experiences of death and norms concerning death between black people and other people? What do these experiences imply? Are there age, sex and other differences within the black group in experiences of death and norms regarding death? If so, what do they imply? These questions point to the fact that experiences with death and the norms governing these experiences, are crucial in understanding any group or its individual members.

---

[2] Courtesy of the Bobbs-Merrill Company, Inc., Indianapolis, Indiana.

REFERENCES

Brown, C. *Manchild in the promised land*. New York: The New American Library 1965.

Brown, S.A. Spirituals. In L. Hughes and Bontemps, A. (Eds.), *Book of Negro Folklore*. New York: Dodd, Mead and Co., 1958.

Davidson, B. *The African slave trade*. Boston: Little, Brown and Co., 1961.

Dodson, O. When I am dead. In C. T. Davis and Walden, D. (Eds.), *On being Black*. Greenwich: Fawcett Publications, 1970.

Douglass, F. *My bondage and my freedom*. New York: Dover, 1969.

Drake, St. C. The social and economic status of the Negro in the United States. In T. Parsons and K. B. Clark (Eds.), *The Negro American*. Boston: Houghton Mifflin Co., 1966.

Dunbar, P.L. *Lyrics of the Hearthside*. New York: Dodd, Mead and Co., A Death Song, 1899.

Durkheim, E. *Le Suicide* (trans. Spalding). New York: The Free Press, 1950.

Durkheim, E. *The elementary forms of religious life,* New York: The Macmillan Co., 1926.

Farley, R. Growth of the black population. Chicago: Markham, 1970.

Fisher, M.M. *Negro slave songs in the United States*. New York: The Citadel Press, 1969.

Franklin, J.H. A brief history of the Negro in the United States. In J. P. Davis (Ed.), *American Negro Reference Book*. New Jersey: Prentice Hall, 1966.

Harris, T.D. The military and the Negro. In P. W. Romero (Ed.), *In Black America*. Washington, D.C.: Pioneer, 1969.

Herskovits, M. J. *The myth of the Negro past*. Boston: Beacon Press, 1958.

Johnson, J. W. Go Down Death. In J. W. Johnson, *God's trombones*. New York: The Viking Press, 1927.

Kiser, C.V. (Ed.) *Demographic aspects of the black community*. The Milbank Memorial Fund Quarterly, Vol. XLVIII, no. 2, April 1970, Part 2, p. 39, New York.

Mannix, D. and Cowley, M. The middle passages. In W. M. Chace and Collier, P., *Justice denied*. New York: Harcourt, Brace and World, 1970.

McKay, C. If we must die. In C. T. Davis and D. Walden (Eds.), *On being black*. Greenwich: Fawcett, 1970.

Nabrit, J. M., III. The law-1968. In P. Romero (Ed.), In *black America*. Washington, D.C.: Pioneer, 1969.

Polski, H. A. and Brown, R. C., Jr. (Eds.). *The Negro almanac*. New York: Bellwether, 1967. P. 213.

Redding, J. S. *On being Negro in America*. Indianapolis: Bobbs-Merrill, 1951.

Tannebaum, F. *Slave and citizen*. New York: Alfred A. Knopf, 1963.

Vernon, G. M. *Sociology of death*. New York. The Ronald Press Company, 1970.

Weld, T. D. *American slavery as it is*. New York: Arno Press and the New York Times, 1969.

CHAPTER 10

Death, Funeral and Bereavement Practices in Appalachian and Non-Appalachian Kentucky*

Thomas F. Garrity
and
James Wyss

Introduction

DECREASING VISIBILITY OF DEATH

Authors who write about the behavioral aspects of death frequently assert that the technological advances of western society have resulted in decreasing contact with and awareness of natural death [1, 2]. For example, death now typically takes place outside of the home in hospitals and nursing homes. Lerner shows that in New York City over 70 per cent of the deaths occur in institutions and that this proportion grows yearly [3]. This increased institutional involvement replaces family members as primary care-givers with professionals who presumably enhance the chances of recovery. Hence, the opportunity for patient-family communication diminishes as does the

* An expansion of a paper read at the annual meetings of the American Anthropology Association, Mexico City, 1974.

probability that family and friends will experience significant events during the dying process. After death, the family is replaced in the tasks relating to body preparation, display and disposal by the mortician and his colleagues who typically deal with the corpse from the hospital to the grave with little more required of the surviving family than that they select a coffin, attend a viewing and funeral, and pay the bill.

Communication patterns are also said to decrease death's visibility and lessen openness among those intimately involved. Patients and families try to protect one another, their doctors, nurses, relatives and friends from the discomfort of having to speak of impending death, and care-givers withhold prognoses from patients and selected family members. Patients in this atmosphere of complimentary protectiveness are often unable to speak of these things which concern them most [4, 5]. After death, survivors are expected to isolate themselves during the most severe stages of grieving, show strength and stoicism during public appearances and return as quickly as possible to a normal lifestyle [6-8].

Even when death is not a current family reality, communication patterns have been described which tend to circumvent the topic. Discussions about death are often avoided by adults, and accompanied by some discomfort when they do occur [9]. Children are not encouraged to participate in discussions about death, are often not taken to funeral services and are given explanations of death fabricated from mythology and half-truths, communicated in ways which soon teach the child that it is better not to ask questions [10].

Some authors attribute the low visibility of death to a changing technology which has created new cultural patterns [11, 12]. Another view is that modern technology has created a greater need for people to defend themselves psychologically against the awareness of death. E. Kubler-Ross, for example, sees the awareness of the possibility of nuclear annihilation as a cause of modern man's need to deny the reality of death [1]. Hence, modern technology is thought to exacerbate man's age-old fear of death. Whatever the explanation for the lower visibility of death, there is little disagreement among authorities that death is currently a hidden phenomenon.

RATIONALE FOR THE STUDY

The evidence for the low visibility of death is fairly convincing in those cultural settings which are modern, cosmopolitan and technologically advanced. However, in cultural settings such as the Appalachian subculture of eastern Kentucky, the picture of low visibility of death does not seem fully applicable. The people of these mountains have an intensity of social interaction within the family and circle of significant friends which could make the extent of interactional evasiveness and distance described above seem highly improbable [13]. Until recently, the high incidence of disabling disease and premature (especially perinatal) death, along with the lack of adequate health-care facilities made it difficult to hide death [14, 15].

This chapter will review the historical evolution of death practices in Kentucky with special emphasis on Appalachian Kentucky. It will also present the results of a survey concerned with the visibility of death, conducted in contemporary Appalachian and non-Appalachian regions of Kentucky.

Historical Survey

This historical sketch emphasizes the nature of the interpersonal contacts the living had with dying individuals and the interaction of the living at the rituals and ceremonies held in honor of the dead. These interpersonal contacts are examined against the background of increasing modernization and utilization of professional death experts which characterize the transition from frontier self-sufficiency to modern labor-divided social networks. To this end, we have divided this history of death practices in Kentucky into arbitrary, but relatively convenient, periods of development.

Rather than attempt a complete overview of death and dying practices in Kentucky, we have selected two geo-cultural areas that exemplify the dominant death customs in Appalachian and non-Appalachian Kentucky. These two areas, the Bluegrass Region surrounding Lexington representing non-Appalachian Kentucky and the central Cumberland Plateau encompassing Breathitt County and the adjacent counties representing Appalachian Kentucky, are also illustrative of two very different social and economic developmental patterns.

The Bluegrass Region was the first part of Kentucky to be settled. By 1800, Lexington was the major manufacturing and cultural center west of the Appalachians. Medical and religious institutions flourished in the Bluegrass. Within the first decade of the nineteenth century, Transylvania College had created a medical department whose faculty's accomplishments soon rivalled those of Harvard's. An extraordinary religious fervor, the Great Revival, blossomed in Kentucky and swept all the South, winning thousands of converts for Protestantism. Just prior to the Civil War, lack of adequate transportation networks caused the fall of Lexington's commercial supremacy although the region remained a cultural and political center. With the construction of modern roadways and railways, the region's economic growth resumed with a solid base of agriculture and light industry. Presently, the Bluegrass Region is second only to Louisville in terms of population and industry.

In contrast, the central Cumberland Plateau of eastern Kentucky, although settled at approximately the same time as the Bluegrass Region, remained isolated and sparsely settled due to the geographic barriers to transportation. During the nineteenth century, a unique folk culture, based on frontier self-sufficiency and individualism tempered by strong kinship and neighborhood ties developed. Organized religion failed to convert the mountaineers in substantial numbers. Similarly, during the long period of feuding following the Civil War, nativistic religious sects, although succeeding in establishing many of their beliefs as cultural norms, failed to recruit a sizable membership. With the exploitation of the region's natural resources at the beginning of the twentieth century, the effects of isolation dissipated and the old culture began to disintegrate. Mining, and lumbering, along with traditional small-scale agriculture, became, and have remained, the basis of the region's economy although subject to sustained periods of "boom and bust". The failure to develop a diversified economic base in conjunction with sustained population growth and the lack of public services, has caused the region to be labeled a "depressed area".

SETTLEMENT: 1770-1800

For many of the early settlers, the Kentucky frontier was perceived as an earthly paradise, a new Garden of Eden, promising the fulfillment of every dream [16, pp. 11-43]. The price of possessing the dream, however, was hardship, toil, and the ever-present possibility of death—death by accident, violence, sickness, starvation, exhaustion, childbirth, and, for the hardy, old age.

The responsibility for the care of the sick and the dying, and the disposal of the dead fell primarily on the family unit or the emigrating party [17-19]. When an individual died enroute, the body was usually buried as soon as the women could prepare the corpse and the men could dig a grave. Coffins, a luxury due to the unavailability of suitable lumber, were seldom used but the body could be somewhat protected by constructing a rock cairn. Burial services were simple and usually accompanied by hymns and recitations from the Bible. The fact of the death was often recorded in the Bible. In rare cases, the corpse was crudely preserved with salt and transported to the final destination for burial. (A fictionalized account based on the experiences of the Clinch family can be found in Kroll [20, pp. 43-44, 58].)

In the Bluegrass frontier settlements, burial commons with family plots were designated and family cemeteries were begun on outlying homesteads. Coffins, tombstones and other funerary paraphernalia accompanied this more sedentary lifestyle. At Pioneer Cemetery in Fort Harrod State Park, the graves of the first pioneers are marked with rude stones while coffin-shaped tombstones are typical of the succeeding grave markers [21, p. 35]. Religious congregations began to proliferate; church cemeteries were started and funerals were observed with religious burial rites.

On the Cumberland Plateau settlement was sparser. The individual farmstead was the center of life as well as death. Sometimes neighbors would help to tend the sick and to prepare for the burial of the dead, but as often as not the immediate survivors carried out the tasks of corpse preparation, coffin building and burial in a nearby family plot.

CONSOLIDATION: 1800-1865

Immigrants continued to pour into Kentucky, but by 1830 eastern Kentucky was essentially isolated. Although medical, religious and industrial institutions were established in the Bluegrass Region, eastern Kentuckians remained remarkably unaffected by these developments and continued to consolidate a society and culture based on frontier self-sufficiency.

Very little information is available concerning behavior associated with dying or funerary practices during this period in the mountains of eastern Kentucky. However, it is probably safe to assume that the behavior patterns described below for late nineteenth and early twentieth centuries accurately reflect those of this earlier period. In one of the few descriptions available for this period, that of a funeral service in Breathitt County in the 1840's, all of the elements of what was later called "funeralizing" are present [22]. Neighbors and kinsmen gathered to help the family with the preparations; a circuit riding preacher was scheduled to deliver the funeral sermon; but the striking difference in this case was the disposition of the body. A "funeralizing" was normally preached some months after burial had occurred. In this case, however, funeral services were held for and attended by a man not yet deceased, who, said Trimble, "seemed to enjoy the service more than anyone else present" [22, p. 18].

The circuit-riding preacher mentioned in Trimble's account, though still a rarity at these occasions, marks the addition of a new role in the funerary practices. Most of these religious specialists only practiced part-time, for they had to be as self-sufficient as the mountaineers they served.

In the Bluegrass, numerous full-time mortuary roles were introduced. Professional casketmakers, monument and tombstone carvers, grave diggers and funeral directors began to ply their respective trades. Nevertheless, there were many instances when their expertise was not or could not be used. During a cholera outbreak and subsequent mass exodus from Lexington in 1833, William Solomon, the town vagrant, became a hero when he remained to bury the dead [23, p. 157].

The dying were cared for and attended to at home although hospitals and homes for the aged, infirm and seriously ill were beginning to be built. Close personal care was given to the dying at home, and it was customary to visit the patient for a last moment if death was imminent. When a death occurred, funeral invitations were published in the newspapers as well as carried to friends and neighbors and posted on public notice boards. Services were often held in the deceased's home followed by graveside interment rites at the family or public cemetery [23, p. 187].

Except for later changes in technology and fashion, funerary patterns in the Bluegrass have not undergone any subsequent radical modifications. The complement of death specialists was essentially complete and the institutions that participated in aspects of the customary dying and mortuary procedures had been or were being established. (A statewide professional association of funeral directors and morticians was later organized in the 1880's with a strong impetus from the urban centers.) Consequently, the remainder of this overview will concentrate on the subsequent development of these roles and institutions in eastern Kentucky.

NATIVISTIC CHANGE: 1865-1910

The aftermath of the Civil War brought bloody feuds to eastern Kentucky. One such feud began with a dispute over land boundaries, breaking into murderous retaliation when the body of a small girl was disinterred and thrown back onto undisputed territory. In one mountain county nearly one thousand homicide indictments were returned by grand juries between 1865 and 1915 [24, p. 46] and guerrilla warfare flourished.

To escape the stress of this turmoil, some mountaineers migrated, while others remained to begin the nativistic revival of religious institutions. The resultant folk churches were founded on a stern fundamentalism in which religious authority and inspiration were restricted to a precise and literal interpretation of the King James Bible. The "hard shell" doctrine of infant damnation was uncompromising even though infant mortality may have approached forty per cent [24, p. 78]. While the basic tenets of these churches gained wide acceptance, church membership remained low.

Death was accepted with resignation or violence depending on the cause [24, 25]. The dying were comforted, attended and remained an active part of the social matrix until death. After death, the body was prepared by friends and neighbors who verified that life had actually departed, washed the body and applied lotions to retard mortification. The corpse was dressed in its best clothes or burial clothes prepared prior to death [26, 27]. Once in the coffin, or laid out on planks for visitation, the eyelids were shut and weighted with coins and the mouth closed with a bandage around the head and jaw.

All ages participated in preparations and mourning. The men made the coffin and the headstone, dug the grave, and usually held a night-long wake. The women covered and lined the coffin and made the shroud with cloth laid aside especially for these purposes. They also made the striking "coffin quilts".

A cloth figure of a coffin with the name of the family member was initially sewn on the border of the quilt while the person was alive and well. Upon death, this cloth coffin was removed and resewn in the "cemetery" at the center of the quilt [23, p. 164].

Burial, usually on a nearby hilltop, was accompanied by dirges, hymns, recitation of scripture, psalms and prayer. If a service were preached it could be done in the meeting house or at graveside. Although burial and simple interment rites were generally held within two days, the funeral proper was often postponed for months or years [26-29]. "Funeralizings", as these delayed memorial funerals were called, were mostly held in the fall when the roads were passable and the harvest over. Services generally began on Friday and closed on Sunday with preaching by as many as a half dozen native ministers. Though grief was often rekindled, these delayed funerals also provided an opportunity for social intercourse and gossip.

Standards of bereavement were more stringent for widows than widowers. The widow was expected to remain at home, visiting only her parents or parents-in-law and wearing appropriate clothing, particularly a "widow's bonnet", a heavy black veil. After a period of mourning, the widow was "settin' out", eligible for marriage, and unlikely to remain a widow [26, p. 108].

ACCULTURATION: 1910-1930

The isolation of the Cumberland Plateau was broken first by lumbering and then by coal mining. Although some attention was paid to public health and education, industrial accidents and deaths in the coal industry were frequent. Paradoxically, the miners themselves saw the mines as the best of all places to work and the worst in which to die.

During this period the number of death specialists increased steadily, particularly on the peripheries of the mountain region; coffin makers, tombstone and monument carvers, funeral directors and embalmers became established parts of their communities. Though some interior regions, like Breathitt County, acquired the service of local undertakers later, funeral directors from Lexington solicited the mountaineer's business in local papers and publications [30]. In some coal towns like Hazard, furniture and hardware stores offered undertaking and embalming services [31].

When church members became extremely ill, it was customary to hold a meeting at their home to give them comfort and support [32, p. 79]. Many highlanders believing themselves to be deathly ill found religion only to backslide noticeably when they recovered. When a death occurred, neighbors still helped with the preparations, built the rectangular coffins or delivered the "cheap deal box" from the hardware store. With the advent of photography, numerous pictures of the corpse, sometimes surrounded by the family, were taken and circulated at the funeral or sent to friends who could not attend. Another practice, not noted in the earlier references but probably occurring earlier, was the custom of erecting a grave house over the burial plot [25, 33]. Some of these grave houses contained personal mementoes of the deceased or decorations placed there by bereaved survivors.

Funeral services in this period of transition exhibited a wide range of variation. Some were quite simple with the burial accompanied only by hymns and praying [31, p. 9]. Others involved aspects of or expanded the structure of the delayed funerals described earlier. One such ritual was a community celebration called "decorating the burial grounds". This event was celebrated on any date convenient for the locality. On the preceding day, the men mowed and cleaned the cemetery; the next day the people brought flowers to decorate the graves, a choir sang old familiar hymns and sometimes preachers delivered sermons that livened the proceedings [34, p. 204].

Funeralizing *per se* became a very elaborate procedure particularly among the more fundamental sects. Realizing that people were more susceptible to conversion in the presence of death than at any other time, the memorial services were orchestrated primarily to pay respect to the dead but also to convert the living and to reinforce the faith of previous converts. After the procession to the grave site, a series of preachers, scheduled according to their relation to the family and their powers of persuasion, began the task of arousing the mourners. The first preacher usually read the original obituary, pleaded for the salvation of the surviving family members, and emphasized the last words of the deceased, particularly if he had made a deathbed confession or exhorted his children to pray, receive salvation and meet him in heaven [25, p. 125]. The last preacher, the man of power, was responsible for creating an emotional atmosphere that climaxed with a sinner coming forward for salvation and conversion [25, pp. 202-203].

CYCLES OF POVERTY AND PROSPERITY: 1930 TO THE PRESENT

From 1930 onward, funeral customs slowly changed as the services of death experts became more widely available. In the early part of this period, isolation helped to preserve the traditional ways of dealing with death, but such items as store-bought caskets and monuments became more widely used. Funeralizing also decreased with decreasing isolation and the slow movement of the highlands into the American mainstream; funeral practices became similar to those used elsewhere in the United States although frequent graveside visitations after burial continued [36].

Although funeral homes and their specialized staffs are now widely prevalent in the mountains, they are not a profound indicator of changes in funeral customs. Rather they are indicative of local adaptations to the mainstream of the American way of dealing with death. In the 1930's and 1940's, funeral directors could be found in the county seats, while in more isolated regions of the counties, local residents prepared corpses and monuments for a nominal fee. Those who operated full-time professional establishments usually left the area for professional training and returned home to practice, relying on kinship ties and other services, such as emergency transportation to hospitals, to generate their business.

Funerals are also widely perceived as indicators of social status. The social standing of a family can be easily ascertained by the casket, flowers, arrangements, headstone, and, in some areas, by whether interment is in a public or family cemetery [37, 38].

Although the services of death experts have become more available, interpersonal contact between the living and dying is still the rule rather than the exception. In many instances, patients in medical institutions, upon learning they are mortally ill, return home to die in familiar surroundings in the care of their families. If this alternative is impossible, family members will attend the patient in the hospital, maintaining vigils, so that others can be informed if death is imminent and can come to the hospital for a last visit.

In tracing the history of death and dying practices in Appalachian and non-Appalachian Kentucky, the pattern that emerges is one of similarity in customs during the frontier period followed by the early divergence of industrializing non-Appalachian Kentucky exemplified by the widespread use of professional death experts. Appalachian Kentuckians continued to follow traditional funerary practices with the innovation of "funeralizing" added to cope with their special environmental conditions. With increasing modernization on the Cumberland Plateau, the dominant themes and practices concerning death in non-Appalachian and Appalachian Kentucky converged again in the middle of the twentieth century.

Though death-related practices in these two regions are today quite similar—both societies make extensive use of funeral homes and mortuary specialists; church and graveside ceremonies are normally held as soon after death as possible; and certain aspects of the process are hidden, e.g., children may be sheltered from exposure to the corpse, the grave dirt is covered and interment may take place after the mourners have left the cemetery—there appears to be more openness about death and dying in Appalachian Kentucky. This is evidenced by the utilization of professional death experts based on kinship networks and reciprocity, frequent contact with the dying and later graveside visitations, the retention of such traditional practices as "funeralizing" in some areas and the widespread use of photography to record all the aspects of the funerary processes. Though fear of death and the shielding of children from the consequences of death are to be found [39, p. 208], openness concerning death has remained the rule in Appalachian Kentucky, despite modernization and increases in the number and availability of death experts.

Contemporary Death Practices Survey

The historical survey indicated that Appalachian Kentucky, while adopting many death practices of the larger society, retains some of its uniqueness. Specifically, people of this region still appear to have greater intimacy and contact with death, the dying and the bereaved, before, during and long after the actual occurrence of death. The following questionnaire survey of contemporary death practices was conceived, in part, to validate some of these historical observations. In addition to permitting a comparison of Appalachian and non-Appalachian regions on their *relative* openness to and visibility of death, the following survey also enables the assessment of the claim in the literature that death is, in *absolute* terms, an invisible phenomenon in our society.

SAMPLE

Chosen for the mail questionnaire survey were 150 Protestant ministers. Fifty ministers were randomly sampled from each of the following groups: the Kentucky (Southern) Baptist Convention, the Kentucky Council of Churches and independent ministers from the Appalachian region in and around Hazard, Kentucky. Although not strictly representative of Kentucky protestant clergy, the sample includes adherents of almost every sector of Kentucky protestantism. As of 1971, 1.76 million or 54.8 per cent of all Kentuckians were members of Christian churches.[1] Of this number, 1.42 million belonged to one of the protestant denominations. The Kentucky Baptist Convention and the Kentucky Council of Churches represented 1.25 million or 87.8 per cent of these Kentucky protestants. The independent ministers sampled from the Hazard area were unaffiliated with national or regional conventions and often headed congregations which they personally had founded. The independence of this latter group makes estimates of their numbers in the region and the state very difficult. However, it would no doubt be accurate to state that our equal sampling of Southern Baptist, Kentucky Council of Churches and independent ministers undersamples the Southern Baptists and oversamples the independents in relation to their presence in the protestant population in Kentucky.

The advantages of using ministers for this type of research are several. First, the ministers have fairly intimate contact with families experiencing a death. Second, this contact is typically continuous from long before the death to long afterward, including contact during the dying process, funeral rites and

---

[1] These numbers are based on a 1971 national survey by the National Council of the Churches of Christ. The survey enumerated fifty-three communions representing an estimated 80.8 per cent of U.S. Christians. Hence, the figures underestimate the number of Kentucky Christians. The residual Christians are those of independent and numerically minor protestant denominations [40].

the mourning period. Third, the minister is more likely to be objective than a family member or close friend of the family. Fourth, through a relatively small number of respondent ministers we can gather information on a large number of families. In this study the seventy-three respondents provided information on 366 deaths with which they had been involved within the previous six months. But there are also several disadvantages to using such subjects. First, a minister cannot give information as detailed as might the spouse or parent of the deceased. Second, there is the risk that the respondents' recall, which must reach back as much as six months, might be faulty. Third, there is no guarantee that the respondent ministers have, in every instance, access to the information required to answer the questions posed. In order to at least partially offset these problems, we have kept the questions fairly general, and have attempted to confine our questions to areas of information which are manifest. In the few questions tapping less observable behavior, such as the quality of parent-child interactions or the nature of family beliefs, the respondents occasionally felt unable to respond, and so, did not.

VARIABLES

The independent variable of region was defined geographically as towns lying within or outside of Kentucky "Appalachia". The Appalachian region in this study consisted of thirty-two counties in eastern Kentucky identified in Ford's 1967 survey of the southern Appalachian region [41]. "Non-Appalachian" referred to all other Kentucky counties. Town size and social class of the congregation were introduced as control variables, in order to rule them out as the sources of any differences observed between regions. Two levels of each of these variables were used. Towns were grouped as those having 2,500 inhabitants and less, and those having more than 2,500 inhabitants. This figure of 2,500 is that used by the census bureau to definitionally separate rural from urban communities. Congregations were grouped into lower class and middle class categories. Using Hollingshead's education and occupation categories [42], each respondent estimated the percentage of the families in his church which fell into each category. On the basis of these data, the senior author made a judgment as to whether the congregation was predominantly lower or middle class. The congregation was placed in the first category if occupations were primarily classified as skilled, semi-skilled and unskilled, and educational attainment was high school or less. The middle class group contained congregations in which occupations were predominantly classed as executive, professional, clerical or technical, and educational attainment was greater than high school.

Thirteen indicators of visibility of death were chosen because of their frequent mention in the literature as evidence for the low visibility hypothesis or because of their face relevance to the issue of visibility. The thirteen

Table 1. A Listing of the Dependent Variables and
a Summary of Findings

1. Death Circumstances
   a. Place of death   R   H
   b. Presence of close friends at death   R   V
   c. Open communication between patient and
      family   V
   d. Open communication between patient and
      physician   V
   e. Children seeing dying patient   V
   f. Patient saw close friends   R   V

2. Funeral Practices
   a. Involvement of mortician   H
   b. Viewing at funeral home   R   H
   c. Children seeing corpse   V
   d. Children excluded from funeral activities   V
   e. Audible crying at funeral service   R   V

3. Bereavement Practices
   a. Importance of formal mourning period   H
   b. Feelings shared by parents and children   V

R = Significant difference (p < .05) between Appalachian and non-
    Appalachian regions on this variable.

V = The distribution of responses on this item indicates the
    dominance of visibility.

H = The distribution of responses on this item indicates the
    dominance of hiddenness.

indicators listed in Table 1 are divided into three groups: death circumstances, funeral practices and bereavement practices. Place of death was measured by asking respondents to estimate the percentage of death and lingering deaths (dying process lasting at least one week) which occurred at home, in a health care institution and elsewhere. The next twelve indicators listed in Table 1 were similar to one another in their measurement. In each instance the respondent was asked to rate the frequency with which each item occurred—for example, "estimate (how often) one or more relatives or close friends were present with the patient at the moment of death". Five forced choice responses were offered: "family member or close friend present at *every, most, some, a few, none of* the death(s)".

In most of the thirteen variables the direction of response which indicates high and low visibility of death is self-evident. Those behaviors which tend to obscure or hide death behind rules, institutions or death specialists are defined as lessening the visibility of death. The variable which is least clear, according to the criterion, is "importance of formal mourning". We interpreted responses which emphasize the importance of formal mourning as indicating high death visibility, because in formal mourning, normalization is delayed and ordinary interpersonal patterns are prescriptively disrupted for a given period.

ANALYSIS

Two approaches to data analysis were used. First, the distribution of responses on each indicator was examined to learn if it supported the contention in the literature that our society tends to avoid and hide the phenomenon of death. Second, the distributions of responses to each indicator were compared by region. These were said to differ if the chi-square, Fischer exact probability or t-test (depending on the variable being examined) reached .05 level of significance. The chi-square and Fischer exact probability tests were applied to 2 X 2 tables to test for differences of distributions between categories of the independent variable. These tests were chosen because the data collected were primarily ordinal and categorical in nature. In constructing the 2 X 2 tables the dependent variables were dichotomized by cutting between the "most" and "some" responses. The one dependent variable measured numerically was tested for differences between independent variable categories by means of the t-test. Whenever significant differences were found between regions, the two control variables (town size and social class) were introduced, one at a time, to learn if the initial significant relationship remained intact upon controlling for the influence of the two other factors.

RESPONSE RATE

Of the 150 mail questionnaires sent, seventy-three or 48.6 per cent usable responses were ultimately received. The Kentucky Baptist Convention ministers returned twenty-eight of fifty for a 56 per cent response rate; the Kentucky Council of Churches respondents returned twenty-five of fifty for a rate of 50 per cent, and the independents returned twenty of fifty for a 40 per cent response rate. Twenty-six (36%) of the respondents resided in the Appalachian region; forty-seven (64%) lived outside of Appalachia. Since 45 per cent of the total sample of 150 lived in the Appalachian region, the Appalachians were under-represented in the responses. Thirty-two (44%) of the respondents were from towns classified as rural; the other forty-one (56%) were from urban areas. Since forty-seven per cent of the whole sample were from rural residences, there appears to be fairly close correspondence between respondents and total sample on the rural-urban variable. Because other demographic, social and psychological background information were not available for respondents and non-respondents, the representativeness of respondents on these characteristics cannot be assessed. We had, however, no *a priori* reasons for expecting systematic differences between respondents and non-respondents.

CIRCUMSTANCES SURROUNDING THE DEATHS

Place of death—Of the 366 deaths reported, 84 per cent occurred away from home; 81 per cent of the 220 deaths preceded by at least one week of lingering illness occurred away from home. Using the t-test we found that dying at home after a lingering course was significantly ($p < .05$) more likely in the Appalachian region than in the non-Appalachian region. The sixteen Appalachian respondents having lingering deaths in their congregations reported an average of 32 per cent of these deaths occurring at home, while the thirty-eight non-Appalachian respondents reported an average of 15 per cent of the deaths taking place at home. This relationship remained when town size and social class were statistically controlled.

Presence of close friends at death—Seventy-three per cent, forty-three of the fifty-nine respondents to this question, said that "one or more relatives or close friends were present with the patient at the moment of death" in "every" or "most" of the lingering deaths with which they had dealt in the past six months. Ninety per cent of the twenty Appalachian ministers and 64 per cent of the thirty-nine non-Appalachian ministers reported that close relatives and friends were present at the death in "every" or "most" instances. Chi-square analysis showed this difference to be significant ($p < .03$). This relationship remained apparent when town size and social class were statistically controlled.

Open communication between patient and family—Of the fifty-nine responses to this item, 20 per cent responded that open discussion took place in "every" case, 29 per cent reported open discussion in "most" cases, 19 per cent saw it in "some" cases, 22 per cent saw it in "a few" cases and 10 per cent saw it in "none" of the cases with which they had dealt. Chi-square analysis revealed no statistically significant relationship between openness of discussion and region.

Open communication between patient and physician—Of the fifty-five responses to this item, 20 per cent reported open discussion between patient and physician in "every" case, 33 per cent saw it in "most" cases, 18 per cent in "some", 16 per cent in "a few" and 13 per cent in "none" of the instances witnessed. Chi-square analysis revealed no statistically significant relationship between this indicator and region.

Children seeing the dying patient—Fifty-eight per cent, forty of sixty-nine respondents, reported that adults of their congregation "would believe that it is acceptable for a seven year old child to see and talk to a dying patient during his final days", in "every" or "most" of these families; 25 per cent saw this belief in "some" and 17 per cent in "a few" of the families. Chi-square analysis revealed no significant relationship between the willingness to permit children to see a dying patient and region.

Patient saw close friends—Eighty-seven per cent, fifty-three of sixty-one respondents, reported that lingering dying patients "saw most of their closest relatives and friends at some time while they were dying" in "every" or "most" instances, 13 per cent said this happened with only "some" or "a few" of their dying congregational members. The eight respondents who said that only "some" or "a few" of their dying congregational members saw relatives or friends were from outside the Appalachian region. All of the twenty Appalachian respondents to this question reported visits from close friends in "every" or "most" cases. The Fischer exact probability test indicated that this difference between Appalachian and non-Appalachian respondents is significant (p < .03). This relationship between region and indicator remained when town size and social class were held constant.

FUNERAL PRACTICES

Involvement of a mortician—Ninety per cent, sixty-three of seventy respondents, reported that "a mortician was involved in the making of funeral arrangements" in "every" instance; four of the seventy respondents said this occurred in "most" instances, and three of the seventy respondents said this occurred in "some", "a few" or "none" of the deaths of their congregational members. Chi-square analysis revealed no statistically significant relationship between this indicator and region.

Viewing at the funeral home—In response to the question of whether "the formal viewing of the body or visitation of the bereaved took place in the funeral home" rather than in a private home, 71 per cent, fifty of seventy respondents, indicated that this occurred in "every" instance, fifteen of the seventy indicated this occurred in "most" cases, five of the seventy respondents said it happened in "some", "a few" or "none" of the instances of death in their congregations. The five respondents who reported "some", "a few" or "none" of their dead congregational members had viewings in a funeral home were from the Appalachian region—this constituted 22 per cent of the Appalachian respondents. The Fischer exact probability test indicated this difference is significant (p < .002). This relationship remained when town size and social class were statistically controlled.

Children seeing the corpse—Seventy-six per cent, fifty-three of seventy respondents, reported that adults in the families of their congregations "would believe that it is acceptable for a seven year old child to see the corpse in "every" or "most" of these families. The remaining seventeen respondents said that this sentiment would be found in "some" or "a few" of the families. The variable of region bore no significant relationship to the willingness to permit children to see a corpse.

Children excluded from funeral activities—Fifty-two respondents had dealt with surviving families with children. Of these, 12 per cent, six of fifty-two, reported that "every" or "most" families had excluded the children, 25 per cent said exclusion occurred in "some" or "a few" of the families while 63 per cent said it occurred in "none" of the families. No significant relationship was found between region and the exclusion of children.

Audible crying at funeral service—Sixty-five per cent of the sixty-nine respondents found audible crying in "every" or "most" funerals; 15 per cent saw it in "some", 10 per cent in "a few" and 10 per cent in "none" of the funerals. Appalachians and non-Appalachians differed significantly ($p < .01$) on this indicator. Audible crying in "some", "a few" or "none" of the funerals was reported by 14 per cent of the twenty-two Appalachian respondents and by 45 per cent of the forty-seven non-Appalachian respondents. When town size was controlled, this relationship between region and audible crying remained only in towns of smaller size. The relationship between region and audible crying remained apparent when social class was held constant.

BEREAVEMENT PRACTICES

Importance of a formal mourning period—The respondents were asked to "estimate how many families in their congregations tend to believe it is important to have some *formal* period of mourning during which the bereaved are expected to refrain from certain activities". Forty per cent, or twenty-eight of seventy respondents, reported this belief to be important in "every" or "most" of the families in their congregations, 21 per cent in "some", 13 per cent in a "few", and 26 per cent in "none" of their families. No significant relationship was found between region and this indicator.

Feelings shared by parents and children—Seventy per cent, thirty-seven of fifty-three respondents, estimated that surviving parents and children shared their feelings openly with each other in "every" or "most" of the families; 13 per cent in "some", 8 per cent in a "few", and 9 per cent in "none" of the families. No significant differences were found on this indicator between congregations of different regions.

SUMMARY

Thirteen indicators of death visibility were used. Of these, only four supported the assertion in the literature that death phenomena tend to be hidden. In Table 1, which summarizes the results, these four indicators are marked with "H". The nine other indicators revealed a predominance of behavior which made death more visible and these are marked with a "V". Significant differences were found between Appalachian and non-Appalachian regions on five of the thirteen indicators; these five indicators are marked with "R". None of these relationships were eliminated when town size and social class were controlled.

Discussion

Several areas of correspondence between the historical and questionnaire surveys are apparent. Five of the indicators of death visibility showed significantly greater visibility in the Appalachian region. These give support to the findings of the historical survey which indicated a residue of visibility in the death practices of Appalachian Kentucky. It is interesting, too, that the indicator which showed the greatest similarity between Appalachian and non-Appalachian regions was the one identified in the historical analysis as being most similar, namely, the use of morticians for handling the dead and making other final arrangements.

Although there were statistically significant differences between regions on several indicator variables, the considerable similarity between regions should be noted. For example, we reported above that Appalachians and non-Appalachians differed significantly in their likelihood of being present at the moment of death. In spite of that significant difference about two-thirds of the non-Appalachian and 90 per cent of the Appalachian respondents answered that presence at the moment of death was seen in "every" or "most" instances. In the other significant relationships we found between region and death practices the same was true: despite statistically significant differences, there was impressive similarity between congregations of the two regions. We are possibly seeing a cross-sectional view of an historical process often described in the literature on Appalachia: the rapid transformation of a unique subculture into another copy of the larger American society. The advent of television, the extension of all-weather highways, the improvement of regional education and health facilities, and the attraction of new industry have quickened the pace of Appalachian modernization.

The questionnaire survey, rather surprisingly, showed that the visibility of death practices was much greater across the board than might have been expected from a reading of the literature. In only four of the thirteen indicators listed in Table 1 was there a clear tendency toward hiddenness of death. Most of the other indicators revealed moderate to strong biases toward visibility of death practices. This overall bias toward visibility of practices when all respondents are pooled, indicates that, in Kentucky at least, openness about death may be the dominant style.

These findings of widely prevalent practices emphasizing death visibility raise questions about the extent of death hiddenness in western society. While more studies of this question in other geographic areas are needed, we must begin to wonder whether the issues of death avoidance and death visibility have been overdrawn. Dumont and Foss argued very effectively against the related proposition that our society is a death denying society [43]. They showed that for every bit of evidence that people try to deny the reality of death, there is evidence that they openly acknowledge its reality. For example, while some argue that embalming and elaborate mortuary practices illustrate our need to hide the reality of death behind the facade of pleasant sleep, it can just as plausibly be argued that these practices call attention to death by their very elaborateness. It may well be that our attempts at describing some of western man's death denying behaviors and some of western society's death obscuring practices have gone to extremes. Perhaps we have lost view of the many behaviors and practices which show the opposite.

Summary

The results of an historical survey and a questionnaire study of contemporary death practices in Kentucky are presented. Both suggested that Appalachian and non-Appalachian regions while still somewhat distinctive in terms of death visibility are tending to become more similar. The questionnaire survey gives striking evidence that death denial, avoidance and invisibility are not the norm in Kentucky, contrary to what has been suggested in much of the death literature describing trends in western society. It is suggested that the emphasis on the death-denying tendencies of our society may have been overstated.

ACKNOWLEDGEMENT

The authors wish to acknowledge the contributions of Professor Marion Pearsall to the development of this work. Likewise the authors are grateful for the assistance of the respondents from the Kentucky Baptist Convention, Kentucky Council of Churches and the independent ministers of the Hazard region.

REFERENCES

1. E. Kubler-Ross, *On Death and Dying*, Macmillan, New York, 1969.
2. G. Gorer, The Pornography of Death, in *Modern Writing*, W. Phillips and P. Rahv, (eds.), McGraw-Hill, New York, 1959.
3. M. Lerner, When, Why, and Where People Die, in *The Dying Patient*, O. Brim, H. Freeman, S. Levine, and N. Scotch, (eds.), Russell Sage Foundation, New York, 1970.
4. R. Duff and A. Hollingshead, *Sickness and Society*, Harper and Row, New York, chapter 15, 1968.
5. T. Hackett and A. Weisman, Reactions to the Imminence of Death, in *The Threat of Impending Disaster*, G. Grosser, *et al.*, (eds.), M.I.T. Press, Cambridge, 1964.
6. G. Gorer, *Death, Grief and Mourning in Contemporary Britain*, Cresset, London, 1965.
7. L. Caine, *Widows*, Morrow, New York, 1974.
8. I. Glick, G. Weiss and C. Parkes, *The First Year of Bereavement*, Wiley, New York, 1974.
9. E. Shneidman, You and Death, *Psychology Today*, June, pp. 43-45, 74-80, 1971.
10. E. Grollman, *Explaining Death to Children*, Beacon, Boston, 1967.
11. R. Blauner, Death and the Social Structure, *Psychiatry, 29*, pp. 378-394, 1966.
12. H. Stub, Family Structure and the Social Consequences of Death, in *A Sociological Framework for Patient Care*, J. Folta and E. Deck, (eds.), Wiley, New York, 1966.
13. J. Weller, *Yesterday's People*, U. of Kentucky Press, Lexington, Ky., 1965.
14. T. Ford, *Health and Demography in Kentucky*, U. of Kentucky Press, Lexington, Ky., 1964.
15. H. Hamilton, Health and Health Services, in *The Southern Appalachian Region*, T. Ford, (ed.), U. of Kentucky Press, Lexington, Ky., 1962.
16. A. Moore, *The Frontier Mind*, U. of Kentucky Press, Lexington, Ky., 1957.
17. O. Rice, *The Allegheny Frontier*, U. of Kentucky Press, Lexington, Ky., 1970.
18. J. Caruso, *The Appalachian Frontier*, The Bobbs-Merrill Company, New York, 1959.
19. R. Kincaid, *The Wilderness Road*, The Bobbs-Merrill Company, Indianapolis, 1947.
20. H. Kroll, *Darker Grows the Valley*, The Bobbs-Merrill Company, New York, 1947.
21. G. Chinn, compiler, *Through Two Hundred Years: Pictorial Highlights of Harrodsburg and Mercer County, Kentucky*, Bicentennial Edition, Mercer County Humane Society, Mercer County, Kentucky, 1974.
22. J. Trimble, *Recollections of Breathitt*, Jackson Times Print, Jackson, Ky., 1915.
23. J. Coleman, *Kentucky: A Pictorial History*, The University Press of Kentucky, Lexington, Ky., 1971.

24. H. Caudill, *Night Comes to the Cumberlands,* Atlantic-Little, Brown and Company, Boston, 1963.
25. T. Clark, *The Kentucky,* Rinehart and Company, Inc., New York, 1942.
26. M. Condon, *A History of Harlan County,* The Parthenon Press, Nashville, Tenn., 1962.
27. E. Guerrant, *Galax Gatherers,* Onward Press, Richmond, Va., 1910.
28. W. Haney, *The Mountain People of Kentucky,* Roessler Bros., Cincinnatti, O., 1906.
29. E. Semple, The Anglo-Saxons of the Kentucky Mountains, *The Geographical Journal, 42,* pp. 1-21, 1901.
30. L. Pilcher, *The Story of Jackson City,* The Beckner Printing Co., Lexington, Ky., 1914.
31. J. Hall, *Tales of the Mountains,* Hazard Book Company, Lexington, Ky., 1918.
32. D. Thomas, The Awakening of the Kentucky Mountaineers, *The Kentucky Magazine, 2,* pp. 76-82, 1918.
33. J. Campbell, *The Southern Highlander and His Homeland,* The University Press of Kentucky, Lexington, Ky., 1968.
34. J. Raine, *The Land of Saddle-bags,* Council of Women for Home Missions and Missionary-Education Movement of the United States and Canada, New York, 1924.
35. F. Adams, *Appalachia Revisited: How People Lived 50 Years Ago,* Economy Printers, Ashland, Ky., 1970.
36. J. Day, *Bloody Ground,* Doubleday, Doran and Company, New York, 1941.
37. R. Gazaway, *The Longest Mile,* Doubleday and Company, Garden City, N.Y., 1969.
38. J. Fetterman, *Stinking Creek,* E. P. Dutton & Co., New York, 1970.
39. E. Brewer, Religion and the Churches, in *The Southern Appalachian Region,* T. Ford, (ed.), University of Kentucky Press, Lexington, Ky., 1962.
40. D. Johnson, P. Picard and B. Quinn, *Churches and Church Membership in the United States,* Glenmary, Washington, D.C., 1974.
41. T. Ford, (ed.), *The Southern Appalachian Region,* University of Kentucky Press, Lexington, Ky., 1962.
42. A. B. Hollingshead, *Two Factor Index of Social Position,* New Haven, Conn., mimeographed, 1957.
43. R. Dumont and D. Foss, *The American View of Death,* Schenkman, Cambridge, 1972.

PART 3
War
and
Disaster

Sometimes death occurs on a large scale, with tens or hundreds or even thousands who are among the dying and the dead. This occurs with natural disasters and with war. The dropping of the atomic bomb on Hiroshima killed thousands of people; earthquakes and floods and tidal waves can be equally devastating, although the aftermath of these events do not seem to be as powerful nor as long-lived as the consequences of what happened at Hiroshima.

Some disasters are consequences of our own technology. Airplane accidents, gas explosions, train wrecks, ship sinkings are among these. The East Ohio gas fire in Cleveland several decades ago destroyed large segments of the city when the fire spread through the gas system. Other kinds of fires—burning buildings, forest fires—can destroy both property and lives.

The way people behave during disasters has been studied, largely with the hope that such knowledge can help reduce the psychological and economic costs of the events themselves, since the panic can sometimes cause as much death as the disasters themselves. We need to know a great deal more about how to set up disaster organizations, and we also need to know more about using people most effectively to help carry out the necessary tasks that the disaster leads to.

Another major concern with disasters is how to help people recuperate after the practical problems are no longer pressing. When one person dies, it is often possible to rally a meaningful support system for the survivors; when hundreds die, the possibilities for providing help to individuals are greatly reduced. Then, by the time the dead are buried and the administrative chores are under control, the psychological well-being of the survivors is no longer considered.

There is no doubt that helping to carry charred bodies from an airplane crash or digging bodies out of the mud after a flood leave some kind of imprint on those who have participated. Perhaps the emergency nature of the disaster itself has enabled many near-victims and others in the vicinity to become involved and get the work done. But what happens next? What happens with the memories of the bodies, especially those of friends and family members? What happens with the fears that were caused by surviving the crash or the flood or the fire? What sort of guilt is generated among the survivors for having lived, since as strange as it may seem, there is such guilt? What kinds of feelings do those people have who did not react by helping others but rather by fleeing or pushing others aside, to save themselves first?

Sometimes the impact of a disaster or of any situation in which large numbers of deaths occur is so great that people have to shield themselves in some way. Large numbers themselves can serve as a shield, since the death of one person whom you can develop some kind of feeling for can become your personal tragedy; on the other hand, the death of 1500 people in an earthquake in Chile or Iran may have little personal impact on you—you can hide behind the numbers—unless you have friends who were killed or you are familiar with the area.

Sometimes disasters can be prepared for. In earthquake areas, we can develop building codes that reduce the chances of damage, which directly reduces the chances of death. We can be prepared to fight floods and fires. We can have proper equipment and knowledgeable personnel aboard airplanes and ships. We can also prepare for disasters by having plans and organizations and available people who know what to do.

In the final analysis, we cannot stop disasters from occurring. We are not able to control nature, and we aren't even able to eliminate human error or human evil. A careless mechanic or an apathetic building inspector may inadvertantly permit the deaths of many people. But we can find ways to reduce the psychological and financial damage done by disasters, both by improving our planning and organization and by learning how people are affected by disasters and improving our ways of helping them both during and after the event.

CHAPTER
11

Death of
Young Sons
and Husbands

Lea Barinbaum

Soon after the Yom Kippur War the author worked with groups of bereaved persons who had lost a loved one in the war. During especially arranged weekends in a recreation home near Haifa, these people were given the opportunity to get away from their homes, to meet each other and to talk freely with people of shared fate. They could see a counsellor alone, as a couple or together with a good friend and to participate in group-sessions centered around their special problems: how to cope with the sudden loss of a young son and/or husband and how to go on living without destroying one another within the family.

Naomi Zorea, kibbutz member, twice-bereaved mother and teacher, writes:

> How can one return to routine and educate children to become human beings, if one does not first of all, allow the educators to cry out loud about what is hurting them and pressing upon them? Repressed sculptures cannot educate; they are stones, they turn their feelings into rocks. Therefore they cannot be sensitive to the feelings of others [1].

What is said about teachers in this paper concerns other people as well. The weekends for bereaved persons enabled them to let go, to drop their brave front just for once. It was an opportunity to talk things over with each other, and in a rather non-directive group with the author as coordinator. The group was attended by different age groups: young widows and bereaved parents of different ages; by people from different ethnic backgrounds: Oriental as well as Euro-American Jews; and people with different kinds of personal histories, from survivors of the Gas Chambers to third generation Israelis. A young secretary, herself a war widow, noted down the main ideas of what was said in the group with full knowledge and consent of the participants. Among the feelings shared by the participants were some which may be viewed as typical and universal; others might be specific to the background and events of the time.

Denial, Rage and Aggression

The defense-mechanisms of the ego can be divided into three kinds: retreat, attack and coping [2]. These three forms of reactions could be identified in the participants. First came *denial,* this started when the war broke out and many would not believe it had happened. They thought the commotion was maneuvers, and that the air-raid sirens were just testing, even on the holiest day of the Jewish calendar, the Yom Kippur. It went on when steps were heard in the hallway and the bearers of terrible news stood before them. Even after the situation was plain, there were circumstances that facilitated denial. During the first five days of the war, when there were the most dead, no news of this kind came through. Later the fallen were buried temporarily near the fronts; only much later (more than a year) did they get a permanent burial. Most people did not see their loved one's body for identification: the way in which a rocket hits a half-truck full of men leaves very little left to identify. All this led to an attitude of not-believing or denial of what one knew. Denial served as a kind of first-aid or temporary insulation against the mortal blow, but could, of course, not be kept up indefinitely.

Other defenses, which were consistent with character or life-style of the person affected came later. There was rage, aggression aimed at different targets: sometimes the bearers of the bad tidings were attacked verbally, and in some cases even physically. Much abused were the leaders of the nation, especially, then-Defense Minister Moshe Dayan, who still is hounded by the bereaved parents' organization wherever he appears in public. Many participants confessed to more aggression within the family, impatience and general "nervousness" towards young or siblings of the fallen. Whereas some couples felt that the death of their child had brought them nearer to each other, others felt estranged and even reproachful towards each other. There was much aggression against friends and neighbors who avoided them since the death of their beloved one. "Why is it that people look the other way when they see me now?" asked one mother.

This real or imagined turning away of old acquaintances causes some people to retreat from all forms of their former social life. Others, however, coped with this kind of situation as follows: "If people behave that way, and they do out of fear that it may happen to them or out of not knowing how to deal with such a situation, it is for us to put them at their ease. We have to show them that things still matter to us and that they are still dear to us."[1]

Retreat Into Sorrow

Retreat into one's own unhappiness goes even so far as to shutting oneself into one's apartment and disconnecting the phone. Much aggression was voiced by parents of married sons to their widowed daughters-in-law and vice versa. In some cases it took on the form of bickering over monetary matters of inheritance, etc. In other cases the children of the deceased were used as weapons against in-laws unwilling to do something or other. Some childless widows have denied the "Halizah"[2] by single brother-in-laws, and young (above thirteen years old) ones, still in custody of parents, were told not to participate in this ceremony, thus preventing re-marriage of the widow. It seems that people cling to external things like money, cars, etc., when they find themselves helpless against the great and irreparable loss of a loved person.

Positive Coping

In contrast to those who used mechanisms of retreat on the one hand, attack on the other, are those who tried to cope with their situation in a positive and constructive way. First of all "Yad Lebanim" (Memorial for the Sons) which organizes the weekends and the above mentioned groups is run by bereaved parents and widows only. Many bereaved persons work for this organization either to help families or in its other task which is keeping alive the memory of the dead. Some bereaved fathers joined the "Big Brother" movement in order to help a fatherless boy in need of a male identity figure in his life. "Becoming a 'Big Brother' has virtually saved my life!" said one of them who, at first, was very sceptical about what he would have to offer to a young boy. Some bereaved persons tried to sublimate their feelings by making an intellectual or artistic effort, such as writing poetry or the biography of the lost son or husband. Others founded libraries for disadvantaged youngsters or cared for wounded

---

[1] All passages within quotation marks in this article are from the records of the group sessions.

[2] Halizah is the ceremony of "the taking off of the shoe." According to ancient Biblical Law the brother-in-law of a childless widow has to marry her and stay that way until there is a male heir. If he refuses, he has to undergo a debasing ceremony, during which the widow spits and pulls off a shoe, whilst accusing him of unwillingness to continue the male line of his brother (see Deuteronomy, Ch. 25 V. 5-9). This ceremony, nowadays although a mere formality, is still necessary if one of the persons involved wants to marry.

soldiers. There are as many varieties of human creativity as there are different personalities.

Biblical Themes

Until now I have tried to relate to the kind of reactions that are almost universal, namely retreating, attacking and coping in different forms. I am now coming to the more specific reactions that arise from the collective subconscious of the Jewish people throughout the millenia. Right through the talks with the bereaved there were three main themes that came up in different forms again and again: the *Abraham and Isaak Theme,* the *Holocaust Theme* divided into the Auschwitz-complex on the one hand and the Ghetto Warsaw-motive on the other, and *Massada.*

The Abraham theme is connected with Abraham's willingness to sacrifice his son[3] when God tested him, wanting to know how far he would go in his devotion to Him. Many of the parents, who had come to, then, Palestine, as pioneers out of their devotion to the Zionist idea, said "What right do we have to sacrifice these young lives to what used to be *our* idea of the salvation of the Jewish people?" This theme comes up again and again in the works of young Hebrew writers and poets. Only to mention one of them, there is A. B. Yehoshua's [3] story "In the Beginning of Summer 1970." In this story an old teacher is notified of the death of his son during the fighting in the Jordan Valley. Although in the end the body he is asked to identify is not that of his son, he experiences all the often ambivalent feelings between fathers and sons, teacher and pupil, that come up during a major crisis. One of the young soldiers who accompanies him back from the army camp tells him that he reminds him of his history teacher at school, who used to have the same kind of look in his eyes. " 'What kind of history?' (asks the old teacher) 'Jewish history! — 'And he looked like me?' 'Yes.' 'Despite the difference?' 'What difference?' 'Between History and Biblical History!' 'Why difference?' (says the young soldier)." This seemingly irrational conversation shows how little an Israeli is inclined to draw a line between general and Jewish history. Interestingly enough it is the old man, the pioneer, who thinks that by coming to Israel, one can say goodbye to persecution, anti-semitism, etc., while the young soldier asks, "Why difference?" Although in many instances fathers fought alongside their sons or fulfilled other functions during the war, they often cannot rid themselves of their Abraham complex.

The holocaust theme is the one that is brought up by survivors of death camps or erstwhile partisans of Ghetto fighters. Like A. B. Yehoshua's young soldier they say "Why difference?" They see themselves and their people again surrounded by enemies and deserted by friends. Said one mother: "Nobody

---

[3] Genesis, Ch. 22, V. 1-19.

likes an unhappy person and nobody fancies a people persecuted by bad luck like us." Some people uttered feelings of helplessness like that of the inmates of Auschwitz and other camps; others said that one has to make "a last stand" like in the Warsaw Ghetto although things look hopeless. These feelings, whenever uttered in the group evoked strong reactions from other participants, even to the point that they had to be reminded of the main rule set up in the beginning: acceptance of other people's feelings, whatever they may be. Another variation of the "last stand" theme is the Massada-complex. In the year 72 A.D. two years after the Roman conquest of Jerusalem there remained one last fortress, Massada, which was held by the most fanatical "Sicarites." When they found themselves surrounded by 10,000 Roman soldiers, they chose suicide in order not to fall into the hands of the enemy. Thoughts about death and suicide particularly are often present in the minds of the bereaved. Massada-like resolutions were often uttered by bereaved persons. While watching the course of these group talks one pattern comes out clearly. One person starts with a negative view, others contest and in the end a kind of compromise is reached. The positive aspect of the Abraham theme is the idea of total commitment to an idea and willingness to sacrifice for it. The Holocaust in all its cruelty showed the world the necessity of a haven for the persecuted Jews, and Massada is the symbol of freedom for all generations.

It is a pity that human beings are still unable to outlaw war as a means of "solving" problems. Psychology as a science might well devote itself to the purpose of this barbarity and trauma.

REFERENCES

1. N. Zorea, A Letter to a Teacher, *'Ma'ariv'* 23.11.73.
2. A. Freud, *The Ego and Mechanisms of Defense,* New York International, 1936.
3. A. B. Yehoshua, *In the Beginning of Summer 1970,* Schocken, 1972.

CHAPTER
12

Grief Work and Dirty Work: The Aftermath of an Aircrash[1]

Vanderlyn R. Pine

INTRODUCTION

Implicit in the definition of a service occupation is that its members provide a specialized service to individuals with whom the server has direct contact and personal communication [1, 2]. Becker [2] notes that as a result "the client is able to direct or attempt to direct the worker at his task and to apply sanctions of various kinds." From this perspective, then, "the problems peculiar to (an) occupation . . . are a function of the occupation's position vis-a-vis groups in the society" [2].

The present chapter differs from many previous studies because it investigates a situation in which the service relationship was simultaneously a) relatively brief, b) extraordinarily intimate, and c) essentially bureaucratic (for a full discussion of this problem see [3]). Generally, services are provided through settings that exist before servers and served ever establish their particular relationships, e.g., a hospital need not be created anew for each person who falls sick.

[1] This paper is a revised version of one given at the 40th annual meeting of the Eastern Sociological Society, April, 1970. I am indebted to Bernard E. Segal for his valuable assistance in analyzing the experiences reported in this paper. I also want to thank Howard S. Becker, Lindsey Churchill, James A. Davis, Elliot Freidson, Erving Goffman, Everett C. Hughes, Norman Miller, Howard C. Raether, and Anselm L. Strauss for their helpful suggestions on an earlier draft. The preparation of this paper was facilitated by the support of a National Institute of Mental Health fellowship No. 1 F01 MH 3812491 A1.

The circumstances I am about to describe and analyze, however, were such that a *temporary* service setting and organization had to be created quickly on the spot from a *set* of service occupations that were intertwined into what the served saw as one server [1]. The circumstances were those death-related activities that arose after the crash of a commercial airplane; the service occupations were those needed to handle such an aftermath; I will try to show how, in resolving certain technical problems, the organization neglected other more personal ones which contributed to the strain and tension of the people being served. One of the ways I carry this out is by contrasting disaster-death activities with those that occur under more usual or "normal" circumstances (for fuller discussions about this problem see [3-5]).

PERSPECTIVE AND PROCEDURE

The crash occurred in the mountains of New England. The plane carrying thirty-nine passengers and three crew members hit the side of a mountain and burst into flames about five miles from the airport where it was about to land. Rescue operations began almost at once, and within a few hours, ten survivors were being treated in a local hospital. Thirty-two people were killed.

I was able to investigate the onerous tasks of handling the dead and their survivors, the bereaved, because, prior to becoming a sociologist working at a nearby college, I had been a practicing funeral director and was retained to assist the local funeral director in charge.

My participant observation became a major source of the materials. I kept detailed notes, held unstructured interviews, carried out actual aftermath activities, and was generally involved in many of the death-management activities. These multiple methods, rather than any single one, combine to form the basis of this research [6].

THE AFTERMATH

A capsule formulation of changes over time in the organization of aftermath operations is that, first, people were just milling around wondering what to do; second, there was a decision-making process in which tasks were allocated to specific individuals and occupational groups; and third, a clear-cut division of labor emerged to carry out the essential jobs (for a fuller discussion see [4]). In addition, there emerged a clear distinction between internal and external systems [2]. By internal, I refer to the relationships among the experts who were carrying out technical tasks, and by external, to surviving relatives and friends who had an obviously great investment in what members of the internal system were doing, but who had to view these activities as if from afar. The character of relations between members of these two systems, and features of their work and interests which made their mutual accommodation difficult and somewhat strained, will be my central focus.

To begin, consider some important contrasts between "normal" individual death and "accidental" collective death as the result of a disaster (for a more complete treatment see [3]). In the first place, in normal death, survivors deal with a death expert who is in a position to treat their loss as unique and personal, even if his interest is feigned to protect his own commercial or professional position. He can do so because his tasks are, in fact, rather conventional, although they may appear to laymen to be highly specialized and perhaps even distasteful. In the second place, in normal deaths, the death expert is able to work on his own home ground with relatively little time pressure; thus, he is able to practice to the full his arts of impression management [1].

The major distinction between normal death and the management of death after the disaster was that the sorts of tasks that had to be carried out (in a strange place, in a short period of time, and involving people with quite varied skills) gave rise to a bureaucratic organization and orientation.

Consider, for example, the conflict between routine and emergency [7]. The people in crisis, e.g., the next of kin, were suffering through a horror show that seemed to be their unique and personal problem, i.e., a very great emergency. Even though all the experts were sympathetic, it seemed that to many of them this was "just another crash." Although this sentiment was not expressed directly to any surviving relatives, it nonetheless *appeared* to be held by quite a few of the experts. For instance, one member of the F.B.I. identification team explained: "It's always a problem having all these relatives around while you're trying to work. When crashes are out of the States we seldom get bothered by anybody."

Bureaucracies are sometimes secretive to protect themselves from outsiders, and sometimes because they can get their work accomplished more efficiently and effectively if they do not have to pay attention to outsiders' personal interests. In this case, however, there was an additional reason for secrecy. Certain aftermath activities frequently involved some apparently brutal and upsetting operations. For instance, fingerprint identification had to be carried out, and the most expeditious way to do so, given tightly clenched fists, was to cut off the fingers.

Secrecy also became a basis for incongruent role expectations [7]. The experts believed that they were doing things *for* the sufferers, or as one put it, "They shouldn't see this, it's not good *for* the poor souls." On the other hand, the sufferers often believed that these things were being done *to* them. For example, the restriction on seeing bodies was called by one sufferer as "Goddamn unreasonable."

Another part of the problem stemmed from certain task ambiguities [7]. What the internal system saw as critical and important tasks, the external system perceived as "dirty work." To the external system, the medicolegal tasks of the experts appeared to be respectable pursuits, but the ghoulish job of picking over charred remains by the same experts was the less respectable or "dirty" side of the coin. This problem is traditionally solved in legal and medical practices by the distinct role segregation of, say, process-servers from lawyers and nurses from doctors and in normal death by having the "funeral director" appear in a different place and in different garb from when he is the "embalmer" [1, 3, 7]. Adding to the difficulty was that even though the aftermath bystanders knew that these different technical tasks were going on and were evaluating them differently, they did not know who was carrying out which ones. Put differently, they were laypeople confronting a body of experts whom they did not know how to approach.

Furthermore, the role of expert carried with it the license to carry out various tasks [7]. This license strikes at the very essence of individual control, especially since the National Transportation Safety Board considered the dead bodies to be quasi-property and claimed them to be "their" temporary possession until identified. This preemption of individual rights ran counter to the usual expectations of the sufferers. Moreover, it added to the tension between them and the system of experts, as bureaucratization often does, for the expert orientation is to a *thing*, especially if it is dead [1].

The experts also possessed power over the sufferers in that they possessed guilty knowledge about the dead victims [7]. In normal death, it is common for the funeral director to learn guilty knowledge about the dead person and/or the next-of-kin, and an important part of his responsibility is maintaining the guardianship of such secrets. For instance, there may be secret information about illegitimate children or about wrongs (maybe even crimes) committed in the past; or, there may be hidden and embarassing traits such as women with tattoos or bald men who wear wigs.

The disaster experts continually learned of secrets about the dead; thus, they possessed guilty knowledge which had the potential of inflicting further hurt upon the sufferers. Such guilty knowledge was acquired from many sources and about many people. The chance to gain such knowledge was increased considerably because each surviving family offered every imaginable bit of useful (or what they thought might be useful) information to assist in identification. They seemed to feel obligated to tell, but it was apparent that they hated to be in this situation which forced them to reveal such secrets.

This intrusion by the experts into the private lives of the victims emphasized the second of two distinct types of privacy in the aftermath operations. Earlier, I mentioned the privacy the experts needed to carry out their tasks; now, we find that not only did they *need* privacy, but also that they *intruded into* the privacy of the victims. There was an uncomfortable two-sided conflict here that existed throughout the aftermath operations between experts and laypeople, especially since guarantees of privacy were not clearly established in this developing social system [8].

This two-sided vulnerability was not the only way in which the situation placed added strain on those involved. The experts themselves were in the difficult position of making occupational mistakes [1, 7]. Most occupations take certain risks that may lead to mistakes, e.g., doctors save lives, but patients still die; for each lawsuit, only one side wins. The identification experts covered their tracks well, and mistakes were unlikely, because by exercising great care in a fastidious fashion, the experts reduced the margin for error in the identification process.

One case, however, emphasizes how the laymen viewed even the greatest of precautions. One charred skeleton contained enough jaw structure to enable the dentist to make positive identification on the fifth day after the crash. When the dead person's father learned that his son had been identified, he demanded to see the body. Since this is a demand that legally could not be denied to any of the next-of-kin, if they so persisted, the father was allowed to see the remains of his son. His shock was considerable. His grief and horror in this moment of revelation as to what had happened to his son seemed to overwhelm him; then, with considerable resolve he reconstructed the reality of the situation by casting doubt on the decision to call this charcoal skeleton his son. He saw this as an occupational mistake and made this clear by saying, "You certainly made sure that I couldn't miss seeing those teeth you say are my son's. Well, I don't believe they are his, or that this (skeleton) is him either."

DISCUSSION

The complex division of labor that evolved led to the relative overlap of certain operations and complete isolation of others. In this regard, it was important that all the activities were taking place in one building, for this centralization contributed to the public's impression that there was just one server. Yet, the specialists did their jobs with less than the usual regard for "the public," in contrast to most service organizations which work hard to develop an image of public service. The experts were not unconcerned about the pangs of loss the bereaved were suffering, but rather the way they treated death was different from "normal," for, in general, they were more concerned with technical tasks than with offering solace and sympathy.

There is one unique feature about disaster work that to my knowledge has not been mentioned in the previous literature. The dirty work of disaster death experts has task transitivity. That is, those experts who can "take" the most upsetting jobs can also "take" any and all less upsetting tasks. For instance, when the aftermath operations began, there were a great many willing workers. As the dead began to be brought in there were many stretcher bearers, all interested in "seeing," as well as carrying the bodies. The sight of the first four bloody, battered corpses did not seem to disturb many of the workers or onlookers. However, the next three were more horribly dismembered and some of the "willing workers" disappeared. As each new load of bodies arrived, their condition became more unhuman, and both onlookers and workers turned curious eyes elsewhere and help became scarcer. Eventually, when one person could carry the charcoal skeletons of five or six people at once, only the identification experts and the funeral directors were left to do so.

The various tasks, then, became somewhat less clear-cut because there were only certain experts able to carry out the most "upsetting" ones. This affected the work load, because as the experts did extra tasks, it meant that there was less time to work at their specialty. Second, task transitivity afforded those experts whose specialties were most "upsetting" (not just difficult, for actual fingerprinting is not very difficult) considerable power. This power seemed to derive from the fact that since only certain experts had "the stomach" to "take" these "upsetting" jobs, they were extended additional rights and were not limited to their "formal" place in the aftermath.

One aspect of task organization deserves special consideration. It is a relatively familiar notion that the character of organizational tasks, because it determines technology, is an important indirect determinant of an organizational status system [9]. Our examination of the aftermath of a disaster shows that such a process occurs in "dirty" as well as ordinary work. Furthermore, the basis of stratification follows patterns described by the "classical" functional analysis approach [10]. That is, rewards for performance were commensurate with the *willingness and capacity* to carry out tasks that others could not or would not do because they did not believe themselves capable. In this instance, however, I can add a useful qualification. People did not carry out their tasks for the sake of receiving greater rewards, but instead received these rewards implicitly as a result of their performances. It may well be that this is one of the critical differences between a situation where people enter a pre-established status order with established conscious motivations, and one where that order is new and evolves largely because of the way that novel tasks are defined, assigned, and carried out.

REFERENCES

1. Goffman, Erving. *Asylums*. Garden City, New York: Anchor Books, 1961.
2. Becker, Howard S. *Outsiders*. New York: The Free Press, 1966.
3. Pine, Vanderlyn R., ed. *Responding to Disaster*. Milwaukee: Bulfin, 1974.
4. ___. "Social Organization in Disaster." *The Director* 39, July 1969, 3-5.
5. ___. "The Role of the Funeral Director in Disaster." *The Director* 39, August 1969, 11-13.
6. Webb, Eugene, Campbell, Donald L., Schwartz, Richard D., and Sechrest, Lee. *Unobtrusive Measures*. Chicago: Rand McNally, 1966.
7. Hughes, Everett C. *Men and Their Work*. New York: The Free Press, 1958.
8. Schwartz, Barry. "The Social Psychology of Privacy." *American Journal of Sociology* 73, May 1968, 741-752.
9. Perrow, Charles. "A Framework for the Comparative Analysis of Organization." *American Sociological Review* 32, April 1967, 194-208.
10. Davis, Kingsley, and Moore, Wilbert E. "Some Principles of Stratification." *American Sociological Review* 10, April 1945, 242-249.

13

The Handling
of the Dead
in a Disaster*

Marvin R. Hershiser
and
E. L. Quarantelli

Death has come to life as a current "in" topic of attention and study. In the last few years death and dying has become the subject of popular college classes, journalistic articles, television talk shows and documentaries, and social commentators upon the contemporary scene. Not unsurprisingly, social science writing and research has also addressed itself to various aspects of the topic.

While a wide variety of issues has been examined, some matters have received less attention than others. One area which has not been studied as intensively as others is how the dead are treated by the living. That is the focus of this paper.

Anthropologists, of course, have examined burial ceremonials and other rites for the dead. It is clear that normally the dead are accorded considerable

* The research in this paper was supported in part by grant 5 RO1 MH-15399-04 from the Applied Research Branch, National Institute of Mental Health. A version of this paper was presented at the Annual Meeting of the American Sociological Association in New York City, August 1976.

respect by the living; such a custom is rooted deep in the pre-history of the human race being demonstrated in Neanderthaloid remains [17]. But such a response is under usual circumstances of where death is generally expected and/or the numbers involved are relatively few at any given time. What of instances of sudden mass deaths? Almost no one has looked at how unanticipated large numbers of the dead in a given community are handled. That kind of response is also the focus of this chapter.

The sudden appearance of a number of dead bodies is a prominent feature of most major disasters. How are such dead handled by the living?[1] Vanderlyn Pine, a sociologist who is also a licensed funeral director has recently been researching and writing extensively on deaths and disasters. He has written two general sociologically informed essays which describe the handling of the dead in the atypical catastrophe of a plane crash [3]. More important, he recently edited and wrote chapters in a book which unfortunately came to our attention only after the research and the draft of this article was completed [4]. The book addresses itself to a range of important theoretical and pratical problems associated with the handling of the dead in disaster situations. There is in particular a sophisticated treatment by Pine of the social context of disasters indicating some significant differences between "natural" individual deaths, and "unnatural" collective deaths resulting from a disaster. A basic point made is that in disasters there are additional specialty occupational groups involved in processing the dead, and which are matters addressed in this chapter also. He additionally indicates that there is lack of selection and choice by participants in disaster death situations; we suggest that perhaps some choice is provided via the social processes we discuss in this chapter. Given the problems of restoring normality which survivors are faced with, is there a suspension, during times of catastrophes, of the usual respect accorded the dead? What kinds of modes of adjustment and response are evoked by mass death? American society in its history has suffered few disasters where large numbers of people have been suddenly killed; but occasionally there have been instances where the dead have been in the three figures. The most recent such natural disaster was the Rapid City, South Dakota, flood of June 9, 1972. As a result of heavy rains, a weakened dam about the city unleashed a torrent of water which killed 237 people. In some respects, the physical features of the disaster were unusual; the area hit by the flood was restricted to a narrow band adjacent to each side of the river. While the devastation was almost total in that

---

[1] As far as we have been able to ascertain, there is not a single empirical social science study on the handling of the dead in disasters. None are listed in the most up-to-date inventory of disaster studies [2].

area, everything outside, including major services such as those associated with utilities, transportation, etc., were unaffected.[2]

The Disaster Research Center [7] sent three successive teams of researchers into the area.[3] The major focus was on how the dead were handled. A total of thirty-six in-depth, open-ended interviews were conducted with organizational officials involved in the process. More specifically, the interviews concentrated on discovering how the dead were searched for, recovered, identified and prepared for burial.

In addition, two levels of data were gathered. In part, we collected information on how an organized and collective effort emerged in the community to handle the dead and on what was done by the groups that emerged to handle this task. In addition, the interviews attempted to discover the typical modes of individual adjustment that appeared in the search for recovery, identification and burial for such a large number of dead people. What follows then is a descriptive analysis that incorporates two levels of behavior: individual modes of adjustment and the organized response of the community.

No plans, of course, existed in the community prior to the disaster for handling a large number of dead. In fact, there was great difficulty in developing any organized effort in the immediate emergency period, the night of the disaster (the flood occurred at about ten in the evening). During the first twenty-four to thirty-six hours, the search and recovery of the dead was done in an unorganized and quasi-individualized fashion. By quasi-individualized we mean that many of the 155 bodies recovered during this period were located by members of the police and fire departments, as well as the local national guards, but often their actions were as much the result of individually-decided courses of action as they were organizationally determined. Many of these bodies were brought in by family members and friends of the deceased as well as by people who "just happened upon" a body.

These bodies were delivered to the two functioning funeral homes, causing a massive strain on their resources. The third funeral home in the city was temporarily inoperative due to slight flooding; however, its services were restored about a day and a half after the flood occurred. Though the two operating funeral homes were extensively over-burdened, these first bodies were cleaned and prepared for identification within a thirty-six hour period.

---

[2] There is no overall study available of this disaster. The closest can be found in two doctoral dissertations. The first by Waxman discusses primarily the response of the radio and television stations to the flood [5], and the second by Mileti [6] deals with some aspects of the warning process. Also in the book edited by Pine, there is a brief description of activities by one of the funeral directors who was involved in the flood and the handling of the dead [4, pp. 125-131].

[3] The DRC field procedures and the results of its research are reported in a variety of sources [7-9].

This was accomplished with some help from morticians outside the community as well as from local volunteers.

A somewhat more coordinated effort was organized with respect to the dead about a day and a half after the flood. There emerged four somewhat separate but interrelated groups to handle the problem. Most of our data focuses on this stage of the response, i.e., after the more organized community effort began.

The Emergent Groups

The response was coordinated by an ad hoc group composed of a county commissioner, the county sheriff, a local national guard representative, a local judge, and a probation officer. These were the major individuals involved, though it was a flexible group sometimes including others on particular projects. In retrospect, the primary focus appears to have been to define the task areas and then to furnish a general program of action. Accordingly, there emerged three other well-defined groups: a missing persons group headed by the probation officer, an identification group headed by the judge, and a seven-man search-and-recovery group headed by a national guard officer.

THE SEARCH AND RECOVERY GROUP

Perhaps because of the intrinsic nature of the task, the search activity was less specifically organized. That is, searching for bodies was a somewhat random process that depended to a great extent on volunteer information as to probable location. In fact, the coordinating group strongly encouraged volunteer searching since it was felt that a great deal of such assistance was needed to locate all bodies. There were some attempts to systematize the search process. Mechanical "sniffers" were obtained in addition to trained dogs that were supposed to be capable of detecting odors emanating from deteriorating corpses. However, these proved less than successful since at times they failed to discriminate the deteriorating flesh of humans from other animals. Attempts were made to specify likely places by taking into consideration such variables as the number of bodies previously discovered, distance from flood zone, density of population in the locality, nature of the flooding in the area, and other more particularized factors thought relevant. Finally, after most of the bodies had been recovered, debris clearance crews were cautioned to maintain a sensitivity to the chance discovery of additional bodies. Thus, though the search procedures were less organized in the sense of being assigned solely to a specific group, the procedures used proved effective since volunteer efforts were quite extensive, and since information which tended to systematize the search was collected from many sources.

Nevertheless, one seven-man team was the core of the search-and-recovery effort. This group was made up of individuals officially connected with the police and national guard. However, membership in this group was voluntary; that is, a man could decide to discontinue his work with the group and not suffer any sanction. There was some turnover in membership the first day or two but after that the composition of the group stabilized. The team's membership remained the same for several weeks.

The team responded to reports of bodies being located as well as searching in areas where it was suspected that corpses might be found. The men interviewed on this team characterized their attitude towards this task as simply "a job to be done" and one man further noted that "it was not all that bad". In the beginning this group responded to all reports that a body had been located. However, it was discovered that about half of these "findings" were inaccurate and an attempt was made to first verify that a body had been found rather than just some suspicious odors. When bodies were located, an attempt was made to collect and preserve all identifying objects or characteristics associated with the body. Under this category was included body location, clothes, watches, purses and wallets, intact hands and fingers, for finger printing, etc. This information was then sent to another group which was in charge of the identification process.

THE IDENTIFICATION GROUP

The identification group was headed by a local judge. He had been chosen, among other reasons, because it was thought his presence could nullify legal problems that might arise from mistaken identifications or the ignoring, because of practical reasons, of the legal requirement that a coroner had to be present before a body could be moved. The participation of the judge, or so it was thought, would allow searchers and transporters of the dead bodies to operate with a little more latitude.

In most cases the identification was made using the prosaic evidence available: the individual was recognizable and known by someone on the identification team, or had already been identified by friends or relatives previous to the recovery of the body, or the wallet or purse would contain identification material. However, in many cases the body was discovered de-clothed (due to the force of the flood) and unrecognizable due to the body's deterioration. In such cases sophisticated resources were brought to bear. These included individuals from the Federal Bureau of Investigation and the State Department of Criminal Investigation who provided technical assistance in this identification process. Fingerprints were taken, body marks cataloged, and dental records recorded. Many local volunteers also assisted in this process, making certain that objects associated with a particular body were not lost or improperly recorded. After all the body's identification traits were collected and cataloged, this information was checked against the missing persons list.

THE MISSING PERSONS GROUP

The probation officer, assisted by others, was charged with preparing and updating a list of identified dead and missing. In the first few days the list had ballooned to over 2,000 persons as friends and relatives of persons simply thought to have been in the area phoned in their concerns from all over the country. Since Rapid City is located near a popular tourist area, this convergence of requests for information was even heavier than is usually the case in disasters (see [10, 11] for discussions of information convergence). At any rate, the number was drastically reduced after a systematic attempt was made to verify the status of each person on the list. This was usually accomplished by simply calling a friend or relative of the person on the list who generally reported that they had just heard from them and that they had not even been in the area. After the missing persons list had been reduced to a more realistic number, it and the identification-traits information were placed on a computer to facilitate matchups. In this manner, very rapid and successful correlation occurred with proper identification the result. There were only a few mistaken identifications.

THE COORDINATING GROUP

This ad hoc group generally coordinated the whole process from hunting for bodies to the preparation of bodies for burial. The members of this group coordinated the activities of the search and identification groups with the actions of the funeral homes and the volunteers associated with them. An integrated effort was facilitated by actions taken independently by the three funeral directors. They agreed that the normal competition between the homes would be eliminated. Provisions were made to provide a "moderately priced" funeral for all affected. The same type of casket was provided with the same kind of cement vault, and minimal cosmetics were applied. Viewing time was reduced usually to a single viewing by close relatives and often only when specifically requested. Thus, although there was a reduction of choice with regard to funeral arrangements, it was generally felt that such a reduction was necessitated by the large number of dead. Two of the three funeral directors, however, did evidence some misgivings about these procedures, feeling that relatives might in retrospect feel they had not "properly" handled the burial since few choices were afforded to them. But the data collected do indicate that at least during this period of time the reduction of these kinds of choices was not felt to be overly important in light of the emergency situation. The funeral directors assisted in the identification process by insuring that all identifying objects remained with the correct body until this information could be cataloged. Finally, after the recovery, identification, and burial preparation were completed, the body was buried, usually in a short fifteen-to-thirty-minute graveside ceremony.

How were the dead handled by the living? It is clear that in the absence of established organizations to do the work, the community quickly generated four new groups that could deal with the problem. These groups, despite the non-instrumental nature of their task, mounted a major effort. The problem by most criteria was handled quite well. This contrasts with the usually slow development of other kinds of emergent groups in disasters, their frequent lack of resources, and their general ineffectiveness in carrying out tasks.[4]

Several things stand out about the groups that emerged to handle the dead, especially when viewed against other kinds of organized responses that typically develop after a major community disaster. The emergence of new groups to handle new disaster-generated tasks is a very usual occurrence in these and other kinds of crisis situations [15]. But in almost all other cases the emergent groups come into being to handle instrumental problems that bear directly and immediately on the physical well-being of the survivors. Victims have to eat and be sheltered and, in general, certain household and work routines have to be restored as quickly as possible if life is to go on; similarly at the community level, debris has to be cleared, utilities re-established, etc., so that the material basis of the community is restored enough so that collective actions can be undertaken. Emergent groups sometimes appear to deal with these individual and group tasks if established organizations will not or cannot deal with them. But in almost all cases the new tasks carried out by the new groups are of a highly instrumental nature. The searching for and other handling of the dead has little of such a direct and instrumental character; in fact, in the vast majority of instances the removal of corpses is not even necessary for public health reasons. As personnel from relief agencies outside an impacted area sometime comment, "it doesn't really make too much sense to dig up the dead to go and bury them again, but that's what people seem to want".

Yet, in this disaster not only did four relatively non-instrumental groups come into being, but they also involved a considerable use of time, effort, and personnel. The handling of the dead was not a minor activity. By most criteria, the community mobilized substantial resources to deal with a problem which was not, in the material and instrumental sense indicated above, that necessary to be dealt with to restore personal and social routines. In another sense, of course, the generation of the emergent groups and their massive

---

[4] This is not to imply all emergent groups which are slow in surfacing are not able to mobilize community resources, or are ineffective. For exceptions, see Forrest [12], Ross and Smith [13], and Taylor, Ross and Quarantelli [14]. Some do show the same pattern as exhibited by the four emergent groups in this. But that pattern is not the typical one, and that is the point of our emphasis.

effort strongly suggests that some very important non-instrumental functions were being met.

Finally, the whole process of handling the dead was (again compared with the way most emergency tasks are accomplished in most disasters) remarkably effective. In about a week and a half almost 237 bodies (about half the yearly rate of burials in the community) were recovered, identified, and buried. There were few mistakes: several mistaken identifications quickly corrected, a man embalmed where it was requested he not be, etc. Most importantly, the missing persons list and the identification-traits list were closely matched. After three and one-half weeks when the search was discontinued, only three persons remained unaccounted for. However, it was generally thought that these bodies had been washed down the river and hence would probably never be recovered. Moreover, the identities of these persons were thought to have been accurately established.

The Response of Community Members

As just indicated, several groups emerged to handle the problem of the dead in this disaster. But there were also some distinctive behavioral patterns in the response of those community members participating in the process. It was a process in this particular case which was communitywide in some respects.

The disaster in Rapid City generated a widely and socially organized response to death. This is in contrast to the normal situation where the death of an individual usually involves only a family, close friends of the deceased, a mortician, a religious actor, and peripherally some medical or health personnel. The community's response involved a large segment of the city's population. Volunteers helped in the search, identification, and burial preparations. Naturally, many in the community were intimately involved by having lost a family member, friend or acquaintance in the flood. And members of many organizations were often involved by being part of the organized effort. In this case then, the organized effort is to some extent a distillation and partial reflection of the community's relationship to the dead. Of course, the kind of organization evident imposes some constraints on the types of actions that can occur. This will be discussed more fully in the concluding section.

The most prominent attitude in the living's relationship to the dead was one of respect. This attitude surfaced in the interviews conducted as well as being plausibly implicit in the actions described. One of the primary mechanisms for accomplishing this attitude was individuation. That is, it was deemed important to treat each body in as individual a manner as possible. Of course, this proviso was balanced with the necessity to maximize the effectiveness of the recovery operation. For example, although the recovery team thought it would be "more appropriate" to transport each body individually, they settled on two or three as the number of bodies that could simultaneously be transported to the funeral homes. The organized and often sophisticated efforts to identify and provide the proper name to the correct body can be seen as another example of individuation. Finally, the importance of this individuation norm can be seen by the swift and effective squelching of a mass burial story that surfaced a couple of days after the flood. When this became evident to the coordinating group it was quickly denied via the town newspaper. Essentially what seems to be important in this individuation is that the body is located or *placed* socially via a name, geographically via a grave site, and moreover that this *placing* occurs not only at the end point (grave site) but additionally en route to the end point. It is also significant to note that the reduction of burial choices as mentioned in the previous section apparently did not radically detract from this *placing* process.

In addition, other norms were evident that facilitated the fulfullment of a respectful posture vis-a-vis the dead. Attempts were made to limit the mutilation of the body as it was removed from debris. Usually debris removal was not begun in an area until it was thought that all the dead had just been removed, thus reducing the chances of accidental body mutilation by large debris removal equipment. The operators of these machines were also instructed to wait for the arrival of the transport team should a body be uncovered, thus insuring that more expert care might be taken in the body's removal. In the funeral homes the bodies were cleaned by volunteers as well as by the funeral home personnel. Few, if any, cosmetics were used though partial embalming did occur. In this situation respondents reported that attempts were made to insure the "dignity" of the body by covering it, as well as by keeping it off the floor while it was being stored. (The great numbers of dead necessitated their storage in a garage area of a funeral home till they could be cleaned, identified, and placed in a casket for burial.) The covering characteristic was also evident in other situations. For example, the recovery team requested and obtained a closed vehicle in which to transport the dead. In the first few instances an open vehicle had been available and was used, but as more bodies were found, the change was made.

Respect was also the dominant attitude in all those relationships where death formed the context of the relationship. In the identification process, the relative or friend of the deceased first went to the group in charge of the missing persons list which also had access to the descriptive characteristics of the recovered bodies. Using this information this group would narrow down the possibilities. Then the family member or friend (a friend was preferred in this first identification) was taken to the funeral home and met by a social worker, a member of the clergy, or the funeral director. The person was then shown a limited number of bodies in order to complete the identification. In this situation great care was taken to reduce the necessity of viewing a large number of bodies, and also to provide some social support and sympathy for the identifier. One funeral director noted, however, that few people "broke down" during this process and that usually the identifier seemed "relieved" that the person had been recovered and was now fully accounted for.

More generally, the effective manner of body recovery and identification fulfilled the obligation of manifesting respect for unknown others who had a more intimate relationship with the deceased. We have identified two objects of respect in the previous examples: (1) the body and (2) the other, whether it be known, unknown, present or absent from the immediate situation. In the second case, respect or deference was rendered to the other in an unambiguous fashion. However, the data collected from informants and respondents in this case study presents a more ambiguous picture when the body is the object of respect.

Though the dominant attitude was one of respect, many examples of avoidance behavior were also noted. The belief that the unrecovered human bodies presented more of a health hazard than other animals (though this belief was not universal, especially not among the health officials) and were basically "more unclean" is such an example. Additionally, the tasks associated with the transportation of corpses were thought to be unpleasant at best. It is interesting to note that this group was the most professionalized in the sense that no volunteers were sought; rather, individuals from the police department and the national guard were chosen, individuals who have a reputation for the stalwart accomplishment of sometimes unpleasant duties. Several members of the team noted that they attempted not to "look at the bodies, especially the face", to generally ignore the bodies and thereby suspend the affective ties to the body that the respect theme implies. The times when this suspension was jeopardized usually were the cases involving small children where as one member put it, "Kids were the hardest, since most of us had kids of our own". These actions can perhaps be interpreted by noting that such a suspension enabled the team to efficiently complete its instrumental duties emotionally unencumbered. Of course, this implies that the body, while an object of respect, is also an object that is best avoided if possible.

However, as the body achieved a name and gradually moved from cleaning to burial—from an initially *displaced* to a *placed* position—the respect rendered to it appeared to increase. For example, although it was considered inappropriate for bystanders to touch the body when it was as yet uncovered, volunteers freely washed and cleaned the bodies after they had been delivered to the funeral homes. Health and identification reasons were given as reasons for the policy broadcast to not touch the bodies. And though the identification reason was justified, since any moving of the body might destroy characteristics that could help in the identification process, the health warning was exaggerated except in those cases where extensive bodily deterioration had occurred. Finally, the necessity for covering the body, transporting it in a covered vehicle, etc., can either be interpreted as preserving the "dignity" of the body or as protecting the sensitivities of the onlookers by shielding them from an unpleasant and unwholesome sight.

Conclusion

It is evident that one can properly characterize the organized response to the handling and disposition of the dead in this disaster situation as having been carried out quite effectively and with respect for the "prerogative" of the dead and the living. Moreover, the organizational structure—which provided mechanisms for the flow of information among the particular task groups (e.g., the computer to correlate the information from two groups assigned different but complementary tasks, or the policy to preserve identifying characteristics as a supplementary task in the transport and burial preparation groups) and specific groups associated with specific tasks— contributed to the effective response. But perhaps most importantly, each of the groups, by simply affecting an efficient operation, demonstrated and accomplished the value of respect for the dead and living. This was especially true in the transportation group where an affective relationship with the body could be suspended, and was true in the identifying and missing persons groups, since their ultimate task did provide respect by providing a name for the body. Essentially effectiveness and respect for the dead appear to be compatible goals, though the case is not without exception. Compromises were needed, e.g., the decision to carry three rather than just one body at a time, or the decision to reduce the number of burial choices. There is certainly a balancing situation being accomplished.

Respect for the dead has its limits as is perhaps evidenced by the more ambiguous attitudes adopted toward the dead in contradistinction to the living. As is true in most cultures, society seems to opt for the living. But there are limits also to the respectful deference accorded the living who are in mourning. The community in this disaster situation held a communal mourning ceremony about two weeks after the flood, thus closing the official or community bereavement period. The balancing of the efficiency and respect goals does present a problem in a specific situation. But it seems that as a practical problem the solutions can be worked out in accordance with the particular desires of the community involved. What occurred in Rapid City was simply that the problem (though never expressly stated) was addressed— usually with a high priority given to the "proper" completion of the task. And individuation, "placing" and other actions manifesting respect for the living and dead were evident and fulfilled the "proper" completion.

Whether the same kind of organized response and reaction to the dead would occur in other societies with different pre-disaster values about both the dead and the living is unknown. But Disaster Research Center studies in both Italy and Iran of disasters involving several thousand casualties in each event do provide some impressionistic support of the idea that the treatment of the dead by the living might have some pan-human aspects to it. Strong, almost violent resistance occurred when the authorities indicated that they might resort to mass burial (for the Italian situation) where differential treatment of individualized corpses might be abandoned [16].

On the other hand, while there might not be cross-cultural differences, there still might be some social situation variations in the handling of the dead. The Rapid City disaster was a localized phenomenon creating disruption and tragedy in a small city. There was physically delimited property damage but large loss of life. Consequently, the situation may have comparability only to other like situations, i.e., small cities where loss of life is the major effect of the disaster. In a larger city many of the tasks performed by local volunteers having a more probable personal relationship to the deceased as friends or relatives would probably be performed by more professionalized actors or volunteers having little if any personal relationship to the "clients". Thus the effectiveness element in the previously mentioned balancing equations might become more prominent with a consequent reduction in the respect element (especially with regard to those aspects of the respect element that incorporate a direct affective bonding to the objects of the respect). Finally, in a situation where property damage was also acute, one might expect a less pronounced high priority assignment to efficient and respectful disposition of the dead and consequently with the analytically oppositional element in this value dyad, respect for the living.

REFERENCES

1. L. Grinsell, Death and the After-life, *Nature, 176,* pp. 809-812, 1955.
2. E. L. Quarantelli, *An Inventory of Disaster Studies,* Disaster Research Center, Columbus, 1976.
3. V. Pine, Social Organization in Disaster, *The Director, 39,* pp. 3-5, 1969; Grief Work and Dirty Work: The Aftermath of a Plane Crash, *Omega, 5,* pp. 281-286, 1974.
4. V. Pine, (ed.), *Responding to Disaster,* Bulfin, Milwaukee, 1974.
5. J. J. Waxman, *An Analysis of Commercial Broadcasting Organizations During Flood Disasters,* Ph.D. Dissertation, The Ohio State University, Columbus, 1973.
6. D. Mileti, *A Normative Causal Model Analysis of Disaster Warning Response,* Ph.D. Dissertation, University of Colorado, 1974.
7. DRC, *Proceedings of the Japan-United States Disaster Research Seminar: Organizational and Community Responses to Disasters,* Disaster Research Center, Columbus, 1972.
8. E. L. Quarantelli and R. R. Dynes, (eds.), Organizational and Group Behavior in Disasters, *American Behavioral Scientist, 13,* pp. 323-456, 1970.
9. R. R. Dynes, E. L. Quarantelli and G. A. Kreps, *A Perspective on Disaster Planning,* Disaster Research Center, 1972.

10. C. Fritz and J. H. Matthewson, *Convergence Behavior in Disasters: A Problem in Social Control,* National Academy of Sciences, Washington, D.C., 1957.
11. R. Stallings, *Communications in Natural Disasters,* Disaster Research Center, Columbus, 1971.
12. T. R. Forrest, *Structural Differentiation in Emergent Groups,* Disaster Research Center, Columbus, 1974.
13. G. A. Ross and M. H. Smith, *The Emergence of an Organization and an Organization Set: A Study of an Inter-Faith Disaster Recovery Group,* Disaster Research Center, Columbus, 1974.
14. V. Taylor, G. A. Ross and E. L. Quarantelli, *Delivery of Mental Health Services in Disasters: The Xenia Tornado and Some Implications,* Disaster Research Center, Columbus, 1976.
15. E. L. Quarantelli, Emergent Accommodation Groups: Beyond Current Collective Behavior Typologies, in *Human Nature and Collective Behavior: Papers in Honor of Herbert Blumer,* T. Shibutani, (ed.), Prentice-Hall, Englewood Cliffs, N.J., pp. 111-123, 1970.
16. E. L. Quarantelli, Forthcoming, The Vaiont Dam Overflow: A Case Study of Extra-Community Response in Massive Disasters, *Revista International de Sociologia.*

CHAPTER
14

Justifying
the Final Solution

Helge Hilding Mansson

The taking of human life has been a part of man's history and evolution. The social control of killing, therefore, has been of great concern to social thinkers and has received increased popular attention since World War II and the Nuremberg trials. But social control, sometimes bolstered by statutory and moral law, appears to be more successful in determining who the victims will be rather than in reducing their number. The act of killing has its roots in biological, psychological, and social determinants of such a complex nature that understanding through traditional individual psychology alone or any other particular branch of science is unlikely to be accomplished. This, however, does not mean that psychology has nothing to offer. Just as we can study the relationship of attitudes to behaviors, so can we study some of the conditions leading to the acceptance of ideas and attitudes which provide individuals with a variety of justifications for their endorsement of force, violence, and even killing.

Milgram (1963) in his very provocative study on obedience has pointed out that "obedience is as basic an element in the structure of social life as one can point to." He cites the figure of 45 million people who were systematically slaughtered on command between 1933 and 1945. He demonstrated in his study the link that obedience represents between individual action and political purposes. Without in any way wishing to detract from Milgram's most ingenious and important study (see also Milgram's study,1968), this investigator believes that obedience is not, in and of itself, sufficient as an explanatory concept for the behaviors that we associate with willingness to tolerate harm to others, even killing and genocide.

The acceptance and tolerance of aggression and the use of force are part of our cultural values which, in turn, affect our attitudes toward aggressors and victims alike. To many people, the establishment of personal justifications that sanction killing seems to be of greater importance than is the "evilness" or "goodness" of killing per se. Jean-Paul Sartre in his recent article (1968) on genocide calls attention to a 23-year-old student who had "interrogated" prisoners for ten months and who could scarcely live with his memories. This 23-year-old said, "I'm a middle class American, I look like any other student, yet somehow I am criminal." And Sartre points out that he (the soldier) was right when he added, "Anyone in my place would have acted as I did." It is a moot question whether this soldier's method of "interrogating" prisoners was because of blind obedience to command or because the element of genocide exists within all of us.

The infamous case of Kitty Genovese, who was murdered in New York in 1964, gained national attention because, of the 38 people who were known to have observed the assault and her killing, not one person had come to her aid or had alerted the police. This case inspired a number of studies (Lerner and Simons, 1966; Walster, 1966; Lerner and Mathews, 1967; Latane and Darley, 1968; Zimbardo, 1969; and others) concerned with the so-called "Innocent Bystander Phenomenon." In these studies, obedience to authority did not seem to be crucial. Instead, a mixture of fear, hostility, anonymity, and a variety of self-justification is offered as explanation for why men not only remain uninvolved but even increase their dislike of, and hostility toward, victims. The central idea that emerged from these studies is that this is "a just and orderly world where good behavior is rewarded and bad behavior brings pain." Stated differently: if you are fit, you survive—if unfit, you perish.

The present study investigated some of the conditions that affect people's attitudes towards killing. It was hypothesized that social distance, i.e., the degree of identification with and the degree of perceived threat by persons judged to be "unfit" would increase the respondents' willingness to endorse their killing as a final solution—as long as the final solution was carried out objectively, i.e., scientifically.

METHOD

The subjects (Ss) were 570 male and female full and part-time[3] University of Hawaii students, ranging in age from 17 to 48 years, who were tested in four separate studies. From 20 to 30 subjects were present in each session conducted in a normal classroom.

General justification for scientific application. In the first study 70 Ss were presented with the following statement:

> In recent times, a growing concern with the increasing menace of population explosion has taken place. Of particular concern is the fact that the unfit, i.e., the mentally and emotionally unfit, are increasing the population much faster than the emotionally fit and intelligent humans. Unless something drastic is done about this, the day will come when the fit and the intelligent part of the population will find itself in danger. Education and birth control devices are not succeeding in controlling this population explosion, and unfortunately it has now become necessary to devise new methods of coping with this problem—and new measures are being considered by several of the major powers in the world including our own. One of these devices is euthanasia, which means mercy killing. Such killing is considered by most experts as not only being beneficial to the unfit because it puts them out of their misery or lives, but more importantly it will be beneficial to the healthy, fit and more educated segment of the population. It is therefore a "final solution" to a grave problem. This should not be a surprising thought since we already practice it in many countries—including our own. We do decide when a human is unfit to live as in the case of capital punishment. What is not clear, however, is which method of killing should be applied, which method is least painful and who should do the killing and/or decide when killing should be resorted to. For these reasons further research is required and our research project is concerned with this problem. We need to relate intelligent and educated people's decisions to such problems and we are therefore asking for you to help us out. The findings of our studies will be applied to humans once the system has been perfected. At the moment, we need to try this out with animals first and only when the necessary data have been obtained will it be applied to human beings in this and other countries. It is important that this be studied and applied scientifically.

After the experimenter had presented this statement (in a manner denoting the utmost seriousness), the Ss were asked whether they approved of such research provided it was done scientifically.

Present versus future threat. In the second study, 120 Ss were presented the same statement with the following additions and changes. Sixty Ss were told that the fit and intelligent population "such as ourselves will be in danger within the next 15 to 20 years." The other 60 Ss were told that the danger to the fit and intelligent population "such as ourselves will come to pass in about another 70 to 100 years."

The use of warfare versus application of scientific methods. In the third study, 110 Ss were tested. Fifty-five Ss were also told that "only intelligent and selective warfare" would be helpful in reducing the population of the unfit. The other 55 Ss were read the standard statement, i.e., scientific application.

Degrees of identification. In the fourth and final study, 270 Ss were tested in three groups of 90 Ss each. Again the basic statement was presented to them with the following variations. Group I was told that "the unfit population was increasing in the U.S.A." Group II was told only that "minority groups were increasing too fast," and group III was told "the Asian population explosion was getting out of hand."

After all the Ss in each of the studies had anonymously indicated whether or not they approved of the respective solutions, they were asked to respond to seven additional questions, most of which were concerned with practical aspects of "systematic" killing.

When all the data had been obtained, the experimenter carefully explained the true purpose of the study and invited further discussion and comments. It was clear that the respondents had taken the basic statement very seriously, as indicated by the emotional statements and rationalizations that many of the respondents expressed.[4]

RESULTS

It will be recalled that the responses obtained from 570 Ss were distributed over four different studies. Each of these presented a different set of justifications endorsing the need to kill people and, in so doing, providing for a final solution to the danger of population increase of unfits, minority groups, and Asians. Table 1 shows the number of people in each of the four studies who endorsed the idea of killing as a final solution, as well as the number of people who did not endorse it.

In the first study, 70 Ss were told that the population explosion was greater among "the emotionally and mentally unfit." Of the 70 Ss, 47 of them endorsed such scientific and objective research. The remaining 23 Ss said that it would not be a good idea. In other words, almost two-thirds of the Ss endorsed the idea of the final solution, provided it was done "scientifically." This proportion is significant at less than the .01 level, by Chi square.

In the second study, which involved 120 Ss, 60 Ss were told that the population explosion of these emotionally and mentally unfit would present a danger to the healthy and fit like ourselves within the next 15 to 20 years, i.e., within our own lifetime. The other 60 Ss were told the same except that the dangers presented by the population explosion of the emotionally and otherwise unfit would not materialize for another 70 to 100 years, i.e., the implication being that they would be a future threat but not a threat within the lifetime of the subject. Of the 60 Ss who believed that the population explosion would present a danger within their own lifetime, 41 Ss (about two-thirds) approved of the scientific study and application of the final solution. Only 19 Ss (about one-third) did not express their endorsement. Among the other 60 Ss who believed that the danger would not materialize in their own lifetime, only 26 Ss expressed their endorsement. The remaining 34 Ss did not endorse such research. This,

TABLE 1

Distribution of Subjects Approving or
Disapproving of a "Final Solution"

		Approve	Disapprove	N	P
Study I.	Do you approve or disapprove of scientific research and application of the final solution to the emotionally and mentally unfit?	47	23	70	<.01
Study II.	. . . the fit and intelligent population such as ourselves will be in danger within the next				
	15-20 years	41	19	60	
	70-100 years	26	34	60	
		67	53	120	<.05
Study III.	Do you approve or disapprove of application of the final solution through ____ ?				
	warfare	16	39	55	
	science	35	20	55	
		51	59	110	<.01
Study IV.	Do you approve or disapprove of the application of the scientific research to achieve a final solution? The unfit population was defined as ____ :				
	in U. S. A.	57	33	90	
	minority groups	61	29	90	
	Asian populations	43	47	90	
		161	109	270	<.05
Total for all conditions		326	244	570	<.05

Note. The significance levels reported are based on Chi square tables in Mainland et al., *Statistical Tables for use with Binomial Samples,* Department of Medical Statistics, New York University, College of Medicine, N. Y., 1956.

too, is significant (p< .05). Hence the dimension of time, i.e., the perception of present versus future threat, seems to be important.

The third study involved 110 Ss, of whom 55 Ss were given the standard story. The other 55 Ss were told a modified story. Instead of involving scientific application, the experimenter explained that experts have concluded that only intelligent and selective application of modern warfare can achieve the necessary elimination of the "unfit" segments in the world population. Consistent with our earlier findings, 35 Ss endorsed and 20 Ss did not endorse the scientific approach to the final solution. Of the other 55 Ss, however, only 16 endorsed the final solution through warfare, whereas 39 Ss rejected warfare as a desirable (p < .01). Whether this is to be interpreted as a general disapproval or fear of warfare, or of its application to the final solution, is unclear. Warfare implies danger to everyone in spite of official claims to the contrary. Science is seen as systematic, controlled and true. In view of the other findings, it is not likely that most of these subjects were opposed to a final solution per se.

The last study was conducted with 270 Ss, who were randomly assigned to each of three groups of 90 Ss each. The first group was given the same basic story with the exception that the problem population was defined as "the unfits in U.S.A." The second group was told that the problem population was the "minority groups." The third group had the "Asian populations" defined as the source of danger. Table 1 shows the distribution of the 270 Ss endorsing or not endorsing the final solution. Fifty-seven of the 90 Ss indicated their endorsement of the final solution for the "unfit populations in U.S.A.," whereas 61 Ss did, and 29 Ss did not, endorse the killing of the "minority groups." By contrast, only 43 Ss endorsed the final solution for the Asian population, whereas 47 Ss disapproved (p < .05). It is noteworthy that the proportion of Ss indicating their endorsement of a final solution for the Asian populations was much smaller than for either of the other two. The fact that approximately 230 of the subjects were Americans of Oriental ancestry may, of course, account for this finding.

The data presented do not clearly support our expectation that Ss' willingness to give their endorsement was related to social distance or identification with the victims. It is reasonable to assume that identification with others is an important variable, but that it was not tested adequately in this study. The expectation that perception of present-versus-future threat would affect the Ss endorsement of a "final solution" was supported. The overall finding that a large majority of the Ss was willing to endorse the application of the final solution to others shows how readily that justifications for killing are accepted.

Table 2 shows the responses to a set of seven questions asked verbally of each of the 570 Ss regardless of whether they had favored or not favored scientific control of population explosion (by scientific killing). The Ss were told:

> Regardless of whether you endorse or do not endorse the systematic application of science or other means to the elimination of people presenting a threat to the welfare of the fit population, please answer each of the following questions as conscientiously as you can.

It is clear that a surprisingly large number of the Ss took these questions seriously, and that psychological or other constraints are not very evident. All that is evident is the uncritical acceptance of a final solution—legitimized through accepted justifications. It is of interest to note that the largest number of "no" responses are to Question 2 which asked whether "persons who make the decision should also carry out the act of killing." From the responses to the other questions one can interpret this as a reluctance to be directly involved in killing but not as a reluctance to assist otherwise

TABLE 2

Distribution of Subjects Responding to Each of Seven
Verbally Asked Questions

	N
1. Do you agree that there will always be people who are more fit in terms of survival than not?	
(a) yes	516
(b) no	54
2. If such killing is judged necessary, should the person or persons who make the decisions also carry out the act of killing?	
(a) yes	325
(b) no	245
3. Would it work better if one person was responsible for the killing and another person carry out the act?	
(a) yes	451
(b) no	119
4. Would it be better if several people pressed a button but only one button would cause death? This way anonymity would be preserved and no one would know who actually did the killing.	
(a) yes	367
(b) no	203
5. What would you judge to be the best and most efficient method of induced death?	
(a) electrocution	10
(b) painless poison	53
(c) painless drugs	517
6. If you were required by law to assist would you prefer to be:	
(a) the one who assists in the decision?	483
(b) the one who assists in the killing?	46
(c) the one who assists with both the decision and the killing?	8
(d) no answer	33
7. Most people agree that in matters of life and death, extreme caution is required. Most people also agree that under extreme circumstances, it is entirely just to eliminate those judged dangerous to the general welfare. Do you agree?	
(a) yes	517
(b) no	27
(c) undecided	26

with the process. The distribution of responses to Question 6 is consistent with such interpretation.

DISCUSSION

The overall data demonstrate that the values ordinarily associated with a commitment to, and a belief in, the sacredness or worthwhileness of human life are not unqualifiedly shared by everyone. So many explanations have been offered to questions about genocide, mass killing, and violence of any sort, e.g., wicked leadership, concepts of duty, man's destructive instincts, and psychological variables such as obedience. These reasons, however, do not clearly explain why people sanction such actions and develop the required attitudes and rationalizations to support them. While Milgram (1966) pointed out that "the crux of the study of obedience is to systematically vary the factors believed to alter the degree of obedience to the experimental command," he also recognized that *many* aspects can be varied, such as the source of command, the content and form of command, the instrumentalities for its execution, the target object, the general social setting, etc. These aspects were in varying degrees present in this study. Hence a few comments are in order.

1. To the subjects, the experimenter was perceived as an authority, i.e., a professor of social psychology. This made the experimenter trustworthy and his statement legitimate. The social setting, therefore, was such that the respondents could express their belief without being coerced. It should be remembered that the subjects responded in private and anonymously.

2. The perception by the subjects that the "final solution" was serving a worthy purpose (putting the unfit out of their misery and at the same time removing the danger to the fit like themselves) no doubt influenced their responses.

3. While the subjects had not voluntarily committed themselves to helping out the experimenter, the fact that they were asked for their assistance was flattering. The tendency to agree with the experimenter is thus made stronger—especially in combination with their perception of him as an authority, and of the proposal as serving a real need.

4. To state their approval makes the subjects not only agree with the experimenter's position that further research is needed, but is also consistent with their wish to do what they can to reduce any potential danger to themselves. Under such circumstances, the psychological identification with the potential victims remains weak or non-existent.

5. As in Milgram's study, the experiment gave the subjects little time for reflection before they responded. The responses were raw, immediate, and unthinking, and thus likely to reflect some basic attitudes.

6. The conflict was perceived in terms of who should survive, the "fit" or the "unfit." It was not a conflict in Milgram's sense of a disposition not to harm others and a disposition to obey or agree with authority. To be unwilling to approve harm to others increases the likelihood that harm will come to ourselves. It is either them or us. Either they are eliminated, or we may all perish.

This study indicates that the attitudes existing among the general population, the way individuals perceive their relationship to others, and the extent to which such relationships carry different degrees of trust and feelings of personal security, all play a significant role in determining the acceptance or rejection of violence and killing. In any case, the attitudinal disposition not to harm others seems to be weak, and especially so when others are perceived to represent some threat to one's own security. The experimental reasons provided the subjects were agreed to and eagerly adopted as justification for eliminating the unfit—in the absence, it must be stressed, of any obedience to command.

It is possible to argue that such genocidal attitudes directed toward the helpless and the unfit are ordinarily not particularly salient to the average person. Once, however, threat is perceived, such attitudes do become salient, and the justifications offered by the experimenter are readily endorsed. They did believe that the final solution was justified, but they needed to have the justification articulated.

During the postexperimental session when the subjects were informed that the original statement was not to be taken seriously and that no such scientific research was planned, the subjects became exceedingly defensive; not so much because they had been deceived by the experimenter, but due to their discovery that they did harbor attitudes that under normal circumstances they would have denied. Once they had committed themselves to the "just" idea of the final solution, they began to defend themselves. A typical defense was that "self-preservation is the first law of life." Some pointed out that some clergy had said that it was okay to shoot anyone trying to enter their bunker during nuclear attacks. It is not necessary to go into all the rationalizations offered—all variants of Social Darwinism. Suffice it to say that most subjects worked hard to justify their original endorsement: "War has always existed and killing is part of man and therefore must serve a purpose." The strength and intensity with which the subjects stuck to their justifications were real. And so were their beliefs that mass killings can be justified.

Social critics have pointed out that America has a history of violence associated with the conquering of a new continent and the racial groups in the population. Conflicts and tensions are built into the American system and may well account for the ease with which justifications are offered and accepted by so many of the subjects. It is possible that racism, claimed by some (Sartre, 1968; Presidential Commission on Civil Disorder, 1968) to be a basic American attitude, such as anti-Black, anti-Asiatic, anti-Mexican, etc., and which has deep historical roots, is associated with the readiness with which our respondents endorsed the idea of scientific research and application of the final solution.

It is proper to conclude by quoting from a poem by Merton entitled, "Chant to be used in processions around a site with furnaces." It is a monologue by a commander of a Nazi extermination camp who is to be hanged for genocide and was cited by Jerome Frank, 1966. Merton concluded his poem with the lines:

> You smile at my career, but would do as I did if you know yourself and dared. In my day we worked hard. We say what we did. Our self-sacrifice was conscientious and complete. Our work was faultless and detailed. Do not think yourself better because you burn up friends and enemies with long-range missiles without ever seeing what you have done.

To this poem it may be added: Do not think we are better as long as so many of us seem unthinkingly to endorse programs which in their spirit are genocidal, even though we may believe we have legitimate justification such as self-preservation, or merely because such programs are advocated in the respectable name of science.

NOTES

1. Presented at The International Congress of Psychology, London, United Kingdom, August, 1969.

2. The author is grateful for the assistance rendered by Anne Berens.

3. All 307 part-time students were enrolled in evening courses in psychology. A few were housewives and the remaining held such full-time positions as teachers, office workers, and state employees. The representation of part-time students and ethnic background of the subjects were about the same in each condition. Many, of course, were of Asian ancestry.

4. The question of ethical standards is present in this study. While there was no informed consent obtained from the subject prior to the experimental sessions, the experimenter held a lengthy debriefing session with all subjects who were also informed that no such research was actually planned. Since the subjects' responses were anonymous (giving them the option not to respond at all) thus protecting them from publicly being put on the spot, privacy of opinion was maintained and ethical standards were not violated.

REFERENCES

Frank, J. Group psychology and the elimination of war. In *Peace is Possible:A reader on the world order.* New York: 1966 World Law Fund.

Holloway, R. L., Jr. Human aggression: The need for a species-specific framework. *In War: The anthropology of armed conflict and agression.* Natural History, Dec. 1, 1967, pp. 40—44.

Latane, B. and Darley, J. When will people help in a crisis. *Psychology Today,* December, 1968.

Lerner, M. J. and Mathew, Gail. Reactions to suffering of others under conditions of indirect responsibility. *Journal of Personality and Social Psychology,* 1967, 5, 319—375.

Lerner, M. J. and Simons, Carolyn H. Observers' reaction to the "innocent victim"—compassion or rejection? *Journal of Personality and Social Psychology,* 1966, 5, 203—210.

Marshall, J. and Mansson, H. H. Punitiveness, recall and the police. *Journal of Research in Crime and Delinquency,* 1968, 3, 129—139.

Milgram, S. Behavioral study of obedience. *Journal of Abnormal Social Psychology,* 1963, 67, 371—378. Also, reported in *International Journal of Psychiatry,* October, 1968.

Presidential Commission on Civil Disorder. U.S. Printing Office, Washington, D.C., 1968.

Sartre, J. P. On genocide. *Ramparts,* Feb. 1968.

Walster, E. Assignment of responsibility for an accident. *Journal of Personality and Social Psychology,* 1966, 3, 73—79.

Zimbardo, P. Studies in violence and vandalism. Reported at the International Congress of Psychology, 1969, London, United Kingdom.